Canadian Stories of Action and Adventure

Canadian Stories of Action and Adventure

Edited by
John Stevens and Roger J. Smith

Faculty of Education
University of Toronto

Macmillan of Canada

Canadian Cataloguing in Publication Data

Main entry under title:

Canadian stories of action and adventure

ISBN 0-7705-1688-2

1. Adventure stories, Canadian. I. Stevens, John, date. II. Smith, Roger J., date.

PS8321.C35   C813′.01   C78-001151-1
PR9197.32.C35

Cover: "Looking Up into the Blue" (1918) by Franz Johnston. Reproduced by permission of Canadian War Museum, National Museum of Man, National Museums of Canada.

Printed in Canada

Acknowledgments

For permission to reprint copyrighted material grateful acknowledgment is made to the following:

Curtis Brown Ltd. for "The Wild Goose" by Ernest Buckler, originally published in *The Atlantic Advocate*, October 1959 issue.

John Cushman Associates, Inc., for "A Queen in Thebes" by Margaret Laurence. Copyright © 1964 by Margaret Laurence. Reprinted by permission of John Cushman Associates, Inc.

McClelland and Stewart Limited for "Stranger in Taransay" from *The Snow Walker* by Farley Mowat, reprinted by permission of The Canadian Publishers, McClelland and Stewart Limited, Toronto; "Triangle in Steel" from *Tambour and Other Stories* by Thomas H. Raddall, reprinted by permission of The Canadian Publishers, McClelland and Stewart Limited, Toronto; and "The Outlaw" from *The Lamp at Noon and Other Stories* by Sinclair Ross, reprinted by permission of The Canadian Publishers, McClelland and Stewart Limited, Toronto.

Colin McDougall for "The Firing Squad". Copyright © Colin McDougall, 1958.

McGraw-Hill Ryerson Limited for "An Ounce of Cure" from *Dance of the Happy Shades* by Alice Munro. Copyright © Alice Munro, 1968. Reprinted by permission of McGraw-Hill Ryerson Limited; and "Red Racer" from *The Yellow Sweater* by Hugh Garner. Copyright © Hugh Garner, 1952. Reprinted by permission of the author and McGraw-Hill Ryerson Limited.

The Macmillan Company of Canada Limited for "Running Away from Home" from *The Book of Eve* by Constance Beresford-Howe; "The Weasel Skin" from *Angel Cove* by Will R. Bird; "The Shining Red Apple" from *Morley Callaghan's Stories* by Morley Callaghan; "My Uncle Joe" from *Them Damned Canadians Hanged Louis Riel!* by James McNamee; and "Hurry, Hurry" from *Mrs. Golightly and Other Stories* by Ethel Wilson.

Macmillan Publishing Co., Inc., for "The Blackwater Pot" from *The Backwoodsman* by Charles G. D. Roberts. Copyright © 1909 by Macmillan Publishing Co., Inc., renewed 1937 by Charles G. D. Roberts. Reprinted with permission of Macmillan Publishing Co., Inc.

Judith Merril for "Survival Ship" from her book *Survival Ship and Other Stories.*

Optimum Publishing Company Limited for "The Bully" from *Gregory Clark's War Stories*. Reprinted by permission of Optimum Publishing Company Limited, Montreal/Toronto.

Van Nostrand Reinhold Ltd. for "Akua Nuten" by Yves Thériault, translated by Howard Roiter, from *Stories from Quebec*, selected and introduced by Philip Stratford. Copyright © 1974 by Van Nostrand Reinhold Ltd. Reprinted by permission of Van Nostrand Reinhold Ltd., Toronto. "Akua Nuten" appeared originally in *Si la bombe m'était contée*, published by Editions du Jour Inc., Montreal.

About the Stories

Supposing you were offered the opportunity of taking part in an exciting adventure, would you grasp it, or would you turn away? If your first response to that question is an inward "I'd take it", think again. Perhaps a call to adventure suggests to you strange new places, interesting people, and fast action—a stimulating change from the humdrum of daily routine. But "action and adventure" involves more than that. It can also mean bitter conflict, the feeling of being lost as in a nightmare, the fear of being beaten and humiliated, and even the danger of mutilation or death. Most of us prefer to experience those threats and discomforts at second hand, through screenplays, novels, and short stories such as those you will find in the present collection.

An example of this frightening kind of action occurs in "The Bully", a story about the First World War. At 8:30 one morning during the battle of Vimy Ridge, Lieutenant Gregory Clark found himself the only officer left alive in his company: "It was sleeting. The air shook with shell fire, whistled and spat with machine-gun fire; and without shape or form, random monsters fell around us, belching up gray earth, gray smoke, gray men." As he raced through that hellish scene to slide into a muddy shell hole, Clark learned a lesson in courage and forgiveness. How he learned it makes an exciting story, drawing the reader in, so that he, too, learns something about courage and the way hate can dissolve into forgiveness. But most of us would rather *read* about that experience than live it.

Or take the case of a less obviously terrifying adventure. In "Running Away from Home" a previously patient and loyal wife one morning puts down her husband's breakfast tray and leaves the house forever. True, her race for cover, unlike Clark's, involves no immediate threat to her life, but her decision to abandon her family and middle-class comforts springs from a sudden despairing awareness that her forty years of marriage have been like forty years of living in a cage. Though we identify with Eva as she tells the story, few of us would risk in real life the penalties involved in her perilous quest for freedom.

Why then do we find pleasure in reading about painful excitements of the kind that we take care to avoid in our own lives? Of course, one reason is that hazardous events witnessed in this way can thrill us without doing us any actual harm. Our reader's seat, front-row centre, lets us watch the arrow's flight without ever being the arrow's target. Still, the enjoyment offered by a thrill free of any risk is not the only explanation. The best adventure stories narrate intense conflicts in a way that reveals important truths of human behaviour. They teach as well as entertain.

For example, Alice Munro's teen-age girl in "An Ounce of Cure" has a disastrous encounter with love and alcohol. Not for a small fortune would any of us undergo the horror and nausea of that Saturday night with its following days of social disgrace. However, as we read the story, we find ourselves smiling, not because we are cruel and enjoy another's anguish, but because the victim-narrator is now looking back upon her humiliation with the ironic detachment of "a grown-up woman" and is inviting us to share her amused perspective. If you are an adult reader, she seems to be saying "Remember how we suffered? Isn't life absurd?" Or if you are a teen-ager, she seems to counsel "No matter how tragic things seem, don't cave in. Even the worst will some day seem funny as you look back. I survived." Painful as the ordeal was at the time, it provided an experience that changed the direction of her life.

Such "turning points" mark the lives of all the central characters in the first eight stories grouped under that heading. Sometimes what the character learns from the crucial moment is disillusioning: surely both the storekeeper and the would-be thief are embittered by the outcome of their tense, silent duel in Morley Callaghan's "The Shining Red Apple". Sometimes the revelation is positive, suggesting, for instance, that fear is controllable, as in the climax of McNamee's "My Uncle Joe" when the boy overcomes his trembling to take the rifle from the men who had intended to kill him. But no matter how the stories vary in the degree of physical danger or the lesson about life that they imply, they all share in common a central character who gains a new insight into life's complexity and some important self-knowledge. Since the characters are believable, the reader identifies with them and shares in that insight, that extended understanding of self.

The preceding comments on *Turning Points* apply equally well to most of the stories in the other two sections, although these were grouped with a further emphasis in mind. The selections in *New Frontiers* show us men and women facing challenges in settings so unfamiliar to them as to constitute new worlds. In "Survival Ship" the perilous quest is literally for a new world on which to continue the human race, one where the ages-old battle of the sexes is to develop an interesting mutation. The woman in "A Queen in Thebes" faces a similar challenge of survival but, in her case, on the planet Earth, which has been transformed into a nightmarish new frontier by nuclear war. The last story in the section, Yves Thériault's "Akua Nuten", also treats the theme of survival in a world poisoned by thermonuclear attack, this time from the viewpoint of an Indian protagonist; and Farley Mowat makes us see Western civilization as a new frontier through the eyes of his Innuit hero, Nakusiak, who becomes "a voyager out of time" on a Scottish island.

The third section, *The Wild in Humanity and Nature*, focusses on the efforts of men and women to cope with nature in its savage moods and to come to terms with the savagery of the human heart itself. In Canada, still a country containing vast tracts of wilderness, stories of people pitted against the forces of a great lone land have long been popular. In such stories the main character is often presented as a very simple person, as if the writer felt that only uncompli-cated strength and endurance could oppose the unleashed fury of a forest fire or a winter storm. "Red Racer" and "The Weasel Skin" illustrate this point. All the mental energies of Hugh Garner's settler and Will Bird's trapper are harnessed to the solving of immediate physical problems; no introspec-tion or humour or conflicting impulses get in the way of the action. Charles G. D. Roberts's law officer in "The Blackwater Pot" does have a moment of reverie early in the story, but he almost pays for that luxury with his life, and once he lies astride that log circling above the falls, his thoughts bear exclusively on the immediate problem of staying alive. These are fast-moving stories in which the suspense derives en-tirely from physical danger.

Two other stories in this section, "Triangle in Steel" and "The Firing Squad", deepen a life-and-death struggle with psychological complications, and nature moves into the background. Although Raddall's love triangle is set in the northern-Canadian bush, nature is not itself a character as it is in "Red Racer". Now the wild country becomes merely an appropriate backdrop for the steelworkers' passions, which climax in a trial and execution on the high steel above the forest. Colin McDougall's "The Firing Squad", which also moves to its climax in an execution scene, takes place far from the Canadian wilds in the fragrant and well-worn coun-tryside of Italy. The wilderness now is in the heart of the central figure, Captain John Adam, a discredited officer who is offered an easy way to redeem his tarnished reputation. In spite of Adam's frantic physical activity in the story, the main conflict takes place in his tormented mind. McDougall's method of narration enables us to see events through Adam's eyes, share his cross-currents of feeling and thought, and sympathize with his predicament. After all, which of us is so strong that, given a severe enough strain, we would not break and run away? And who can be sure that he might not be tempted to sacrifice the life of a fellow human being to save himself?

The best action-adventure fiction engages our deeper emotions and makes us ask such questions. At the same time, as the stories carry us away to other places, other times, they take us on a journey inward to confront ourselves.

John Stevens
Roger Smith

Contents

The Wild in Humanity and Nature

Turning Points

The Outlaw

Sinclair Ross

She was beautiful but dangerous. She had thrown one man and killed him, thrown another and broken his collar bone, and my parents, as if they knew what the sight of her idle in her stall was doing to me, never let a day go by without giving lurid details, everything from splints and stitches to the undertaker, of the painful and untimely end in store for me should I ever take it into my fool young head to try to ride her.

"I've got troubles enough without having you laid up with broken bones and doctor bills. She's a sly one, mind, and no good's ever come of her."

"Besides, you're only turned thirteen, and a grown man, a regular cowboy at that, would think twice before tackling her. Another year and then we'll see. You'll both be that much older. In the meantime nobody expects it of you."

In the meantime, though, she was a captive, pining her heart away. Week after week she stamped and pawed, nosed the hay out of her manger contemptuously, flung up her head and poured out wild, despairing neighs into the prairie winds and blizzards streaming past. It was mostly, of course, for my benefit. She had sized me up, evidently, as soft-hearted as well as faint-hearted, and decided there was just a chance that I might weaken and go riding. Her neighs, just as she intended they should, tormented and shamed me.

She was a good horse, but a reprobate. That was how we came to own her. At the auction sale where she was put up, her reputation as a killer spread among the crowd, and my father got her cheap. He was such a practical, level-headed man, and she was so obviously a poor investment, that I suspect it was because of me he bought her. As I stood at his side in the front row of the crowd and watched them lead her out, poised, dramatic, radiant, some of the sudden desire that overwhelmed me must have leaped from my face and melted him.

"Anyway, she's a bargain," he defended himself that evening at the supper table. "I can always sell her and at least get back what I paid. But first I want to see what a taste of good hard work will do."

He tried it. His intention was to work her on the land a month or two, just till she was tamed down to make an all-round, serviceable saddle horse, but after a painful week of half-days on the plow he let her keep her stall. She was too hard on his nerves, he said, straining ahead and pulling twice her share. She was too hard on his self-respect, actually, the slender limbs, the imperious head.

For she was a very lovely reprobate. Twenty years of struggle with the land had made him a determined, often hard man, but he couldn't bring himself to break her spirit with the plow.

She was one horse, and she was all horses. Thundering battle chargers, fleet Arabians, untamed mustangs — sitting beside her on her manger I knew and rode them all. There was history in her shapely head and burning eyes. I charged with her at Balaklava, Waterloo, scoured the deserts of Africa and the steppes of the Ukraine. Conquest and carnage, trumpets and glory — she understood, and carried me triumphantly.

To approach her was to be enlarged, transported. She was

coal-black, gleaming, queenly. Her mane had a ripple and her neck an arch. And somehow, softly and mysteriously, she was always burning. The reflection on her glossy hide, whether of winter sunshine or yellow lantern light, seemed the glow of some fierce, secret passion. There were moments when I felt the whole stable charged with her, as if she were the priestess of her kind, in communion with her deity.

For all that, though, she was a very dangerous horse, and dutifully my parents kept warning me. Facts didn't lie, they pointed out. A record was a record.

Isabel did her utmost to convince me that the record was a slander. With nuzzling, velvet lips she coaxed and pleaded, whispered that the delights of fantasy and dream were but as shadows beside the exhilarations of reality. Only try reality — slip her bridle on. Only be reasonable — ask myself what she would gain by throwing me. After all, I was turned thirteen. It wasn't as if I were a *small* boy.

And then, temptress, she bore me off to the mountain top of my vanity, and with all the world spread out before my gaze, talked guilefully of prestige and acclaim.

Over there, three miles away, was the school house. What a sensation to come galloping up on her, the notorious outlaw, instead of jogging along as usual on bandy-legged old Pete. What a surprise for Millie Dickson, whose efforts to be loyal to me were always defeated by my lack of verve and daring. For it was true: on the playground I had only a fair rating. I was butterfingers when it came to ball, and once in a fight I had cravenly turned tail and run. How sweet to wipe out all the ignominy of my past, to be deferred to by the older boys, to bask in Millie's smiles of favour.

And over there, seven miles away, the cupolas of its grain elevators just visible on the horizon, was town. Where fairs were sometimes held, and races run. On such a horse I naturally would win, and for all I knew the prize might be a hundred dollars. Well, then — supposing I could treat Millie to ice-cream *and* a movie!

Here Isabel would pause a moment, contemptuous of one so craven, then whinny shrill in challenge to some other rider, with heart and spirit equal to her own. There was no one, of course, to hear the challenge, but still it always troubled me. Johnny Olsen, for instance, the show-off Swede who had punched my nose and made me run—supposing he should come along and say, "I'll ride her for you—I'm not scared!" What kind of figure then would I cut? What would Millie Dickson say?

Isabel's motives, in all this, were two. The first was a natural, purely equine desire to escape from her stall and stretch her legs. The second, equally strong, was a perverse, purely feminine itch to bend me to her will.

For it was a will as imperious as her head. Her pride was at stake; I had to be reduced. With the first coaxing nuzzle of her lips she had committed herself to the struggle, and that as a male I was still at such a rudimentary stage made it doubly imperative that she emerge the victor. Defeat by a man would have been defeat, bitter but endurable. Defeat by a boy, on the other hand, would have been sheer humiliation.

On account of the roads and weather school was closed for two months after Christmas, and as the winter wore on it became increasingly difficult to resist her. A good deal of the time my father was away with wheat to town, and it was three miles to the nearest neighbour where there was another boy. I had chores, books, and the toolshed to keep me busy, but still there were long hours of idleness. Hungry for companionship, it was only natural that I should turn to Isabel. There were always her tail and mane to comb when we wearied of each other conversationally.

My association with her, of course, was virtual disobedience. I knew that she was charging me with desire, that eventually under its pressure I must burst like a blister, but still, despite conscience and good intentions, I lingered. Leaving her was always difficult, like leaving a fair or picnic, and going home to hunt the cows.

And then one clear sharp day, early in February, Millie Dickson and her mother drove over to spend the afternoon, and suddenly the temptation was too much for me.

They came early, country-fashion, so that Mrs. Dickson would have time for a long talk and tea, and be home again before nightfall. My father was away to town, and when they drove up in their bright red cutter I hurried out to take the horse. Mrs. Dickson was generous in her thanks, and even Millie smiled invitingly from beneath her frosted yellow curls. She had always liked me well enough. It was just that my behaviour at school made it difficult to be my champion.

I was shy when I returned to the house, but exceedingly happy. We all sat in the kitchen, not only because it was the largest, warmest room, but also because it gave my mother a chance to entertain her guest and at the same time whip up fresh biscuits and a cake in their honour. Mrs. Dickson asked so many friendly questions that I squirmed with pleasure till the varnish on my chair was fairly blistered. What could it mean but that at home Millie did champion me, that she suppressed the discreditable and spoke only of the best?

She and I talked, too. We leafed through old magazines, gossiped about school, speculated on the new teacher, and gradually established a sense of intimacy and good will that made me confident my past was all forgotten, my future rosy and secure. For an hour it was like that — socially the most gratifying hour I had ever spent — and then, as nearly always happened when my mother had visitors, the delinquencies and scandals of the community moved in, and the kitchen became a place unfit for innocent young ears.

There must have been a considerable number of these delinquencies. It was indeed a very upright, fine community, but it must have had its wayward side. Anyway, surveying my entire boyhood, I am sure I could count on the fingers of one hand the times I was *not* sent out to chop wood or look for eggs when my mother and her friends got started on the neighbours. Usually I had a fair idea from the thread of conversation who it was who had been up to what, but this time, absorbed in my relationship with Millie, I heard nothing till my mother tapped my shoulder.

"Come along," she said brightly, affecting concern for our

appetites and health. "It's too fine a day for you and Millie to be sitting in the house. Run out and play in the fresh air, so you'll be ready for your tea."

But at thirteen you don't play with a girl. You can neither skin the cat with her up in the loft among the rafters, nor turn somersaults down a strawstack. I did suggest taking the .22 and going after rabbits, but the dear little bunnies were so sweet, she said, she couldn't bear to hurt them. Naturally, therefore, after a chilly and dispiriting turn or two around the barnyard, I took her in to visit Isabel.

Isabel rose to the occasion. She minced and pawed, strained at her halter shank to let us see how badly she wanted to be taken out, then nipped our sleeves to prove her gentle playfulness. And finally, to remind us that despite such intimacies she was by no means an ordinary horse, she lifted her head and trumpeted out one of her wild, dramatic neighs.

Millie was impressed. "The wonderful way she holds her head," she said, "just like a picture. If only you could ride her to school."

"Nobody rides her — anywhere," I replied curtly. "She's an outlaw." And then, as her mouth drooped in disappointment, "At least nobody's *supposed* to ride her."

She jumped for it. "You mean you do ride her? And she doesn't throw you?"

"Of course," I conceded modestly, "she's very easy to ride. Such speed—and smooth as a rocking chair. When you look down the ground's just like water running past. But she could throw me all right if she had a mind to."

Millie sighed. "I'd like so much though to *see* you ride her. Today — isn't it a good chance, with them in there talking and your father away to town?"

I hesitated, overcome by a feeling of fright and commitment, and then Isabel too joined in. She begged and wheedled, looked so innocent, at the same time so hurt and disappointed, that Millie exclaimed she felt like going for a ride herself. And that settled it. "Stand at the door and see no one's coming," I commanded. "I'll put her bridle on."

Isabel practically put it on herself. She gave a shrill, excited whinny as I led her out, pranced like a circus pony, pushed me along still faster with her nose. "No," I answered Millie shortly, "I don't use the saddle. You don't get sore, she rides so easy. And in case she turns mean I won't get tangled in the stirrups."

With a flutter in her voice Millie said, "Do you really think you should?" and in response I steeled myself, nonchalantly turned up the collar of my sheepskin. "At the rate she goes," I explained, "the wind cuts through you like a knife."

To myself I reflected, "There's plenty of snow. At the worst it will only be a spill."

Isabel stood quite still till I was mounted. She even stood still a moment longer, letting me gather myself, take a firm grip of the reins, crouch low in readiness. Then with a plunge, a spasm of muscles, she was off. And it was true: the wind cut sharp and bitter like a knife, the snow slipped past like water. Only in her motion there was a difference. She was like a rocket, not a rocking chair.

It was nearly a mile, though, before I began properly to understand what was happening. Isabel the outlaw — the horse that had killed a man, that people talked about for fifty miles — here was I, just turned thirteen, and riding her. And an immense pride filled me. Cold as I was I pushed my sheepskin collar down and straightened recklessly to feel the rush of wind. I needed it that way, a counteracting sting of cold to steady the exhilaration.

We had gone another mile before I remembered Millie, and at once, as if sensitive to my concern, Isabel drew up short for breath. She didn't drop to a trot or walk as an ordinary horse would have done, but instead, with the clean grace and precision of a bird alighting on a branch, came smoothly to a halt. And for a moment or two, before starting home again, she rested. The prairie spread before us cold and sparkling in the winter sunlight, and poised and motionless, ears pricked forwards, nostrils faintly quivering, she breathed in rapturously its loping miles of freedom.

And I too, responsive to her bidding, was aware as never before of its austere, unrelenting beauty. There were the white fields and the blue, metallic sky; the little splashes here and there of yellow strawstack, luminous and clear as drops of gum on fresh pine lumber; the scattered farmsteads brave and wistful in their isolation; the gleam of sun and snow. I wanted none of it, but she insisted. Thirteen years old and riding an outlaw — naturally I wanted only that. I wanted to indulge shamelessly my vanity, to drink the daring and success of my exploit in full-strength draughts, but Isabel, like a conscientious teacher at a fair, dragging you off to see instructive things, insisted on the landscape.

Look, she said firmly, while it's here before you, so that to the last detail it will remain clear. For you, too, some day there may be stalls and halters, and it will be a good memory.

But only for a moment or two, and then we were off again. She went even faster going home. She disdained and rebelled against her stall, but the way she whipped the wind around my ears you would have thought she had suddenly conceived a great affection for it. It was a strong wind, fiercely cold. There was a sharp sting in my ears a minute, then a sudden warmth and ease. I knew they were frozen, but there wasn't time to worry. I worked my collar up, crouched low again. Her mane blew back and lashed my face. Before the steady blast of wind my forehead felt as if the bone were wearing thin. But I didn't mind. I was riding her and holding on. I felt fearless, proud, mature. All the shame and misgivings of the past were over. I was now both her master and my own.

And then she was fifteen or twenty feet away, demurely watching me, and I was picking myself up and spitting snow.

She had done it with the utmost skill, right head first into a snowdrift, where I wouldn't hurt myself, less than a quarter of a mile from home.

And not even to toss her head and gallop off so that Millie would think she had done it in a fit of fright or meanness. Just to stand there, a picture of puzzled innocence, blandly transferring all the blame on me. What was wrong? Just when we were getting on so splendidly—why on earth had I deserted her?

For in her own way, despite her record, Isabel was something of a moralist. She took a firm stand against pride that wasn't justified. She considered my use of the word "master" insufferably presumptuous. Being able to ride an outlaw was not the same thing at all as being accorded the privilege of riding one, and for the good of my soul, it was high time I appreciated the distinction.

She stood still, sniffing in my direction, until I had almost reached her, then gave a disdainful snort and trotted pertly home. At the stable door she was waiting for me. I approached limping — not because I was hurt, but because with Millie standing back a little distance, goggle-eyed, I felt it looked better, made my tumble less an occasion for laughter — and as if believing me Isabel thrust her nose out, all condolence, and felt me tenderly where I was pretending it was sore. From the bottom of her heart she hoped I wouldn't be so unfortunate another time. So far as she was concerned, however, she could make no promises. There had been one fall, she explained to Millie, and there might easily be another. The future was entirely up to me. She couldn't be responsible for my horsemanship.

"Your ears are frozen," Millie changed the subject. "And your mother knows everything — she's going to let your father handle you."

I looked at her accusingly, but in a smug, self-righteous tone she explained, "She called you twice, and then came out to see why you didn't answer. Just in time to see it happen. I'll rub your ears with snow if you like before we go in for tea."

It was a good tea, but I didn't eat much. My ears were not only swelling badly and turning purple; they were also starting to drip. My mother pinned a wash cloth to each shoulder, then sprinkled on talcum powder. She said nothing, but was ominously white-lipped and calm—saving herself up, I didn't doubt, until we were alone. I was in misery to escape upstairs to a mirror, but she insisted, probably as a kind of punishment, that I stay and finish my tea. Millie, I noticed, didn't eat much either, and kept her eyes turned fastidiously away.

When finally Mrs. Dickson and Millie were gone—and as an additional humiliation, I wasn't allowed out to bring round their horse — my mother replaced the wash cloths with towels. Still silent, still white-lipped, and since there was no need, now that we were alone, for her to keep on saving herself up, it struck me that perhaps the condition of my ears was really serious.

"They're smarting bad—and throbbing," I said hopefully. "It must have been colder than I thought."

"It must have been," she agreed. "Go up to your room now out of my way till suppertime. I'd better talk to your father before he sees you anyway."

I knew then that she was as afraid of what was in store for me as I was. Her expression remained stern, but there was a softness in her voice, a note of anxiety. It was a good sign, but it was also a bad one. It meant that she expected my father's anger to be explosive and extreme.

Upstairs, swollen and tender as they were, I gave my ears a brisk rubbing. They were already dripping and unsightly. A little worse, a darker, a more alarming purple, and they might get me out of a hiding.

While waiting I also rehearsed a number of entrances, a number of defences, but at the last minute abandoned all of them. The heat in my ears as I went downstairs was spreading like a prairie fire, and when I entered the kitchen there was such a blaze of it across my eyes that I could make out my father only as a vague, menacing form. A desperate resolve seized me; should he so much as threaten the razor strap I would ride away on Isabel and be lost to them forever.

But instead of pouncing he looked me over critically a minute, then hitched in his chair to the table and began buttering a piece of bread. "Some bronco buster," he said at last, in a weary, disillusioned voice. "All you need now is a ten-gallon."

"I didn't have the saddle — and she stopped short and shied." My voice climbed defensively. In dramatization of the suddenness of the stop I drove a clenched fist into an open palm. "I had been sticking on all right though — for four miles or more."

"Anyway," he said resignedly, "you've got yourself a pretty pair of ears."

I raised a quick, self-conscious hand to touch them, and my mother assured me, "They're still there all right—don't worry. They made a hit with Millie too, judging by the look on her face. I think she'll be seeing them tonight in her sleep."

"But the mare," my father interrupted in a man-to-man tone of voice, abruptly cold-shouldering my mother, "how did you find her? Mean as she's supposed to be?"

"Not mean at all. Even when I was getting on—she stood and let me."

"Next time, just the same, you'd better play safe and use a snaffle. I'll hunt one up for you. It won't hurt her so long as she behaves."

"The next time!" my mother cried. "Talking about the next time when you ought to be taking down his breeches. She's no fit horse for a boy. If nobody'll buy her you ought to give her away, before she breaks somebody else's neck."

She went on a long time like that, but I didn't pay much attention. Pride—that was what it amounted to—pride even greater than mine had been before I landed in the snowdrift. It sent me soaring a minute, took my breath away, but it also brought a little shiver of embarrassment and shame. How long, then, had I kept them waiting? How many times in the last few months had they looked at me and despaired?

"One thing," my mother declared with finality, "you're not riding her to school. The things I'd be thinking and seeing all day—I just couldn't stand it."

"You hear," my father agreed. "I'll not have you carrying on with a lot of young fools crazy as yourself—being a good fellow, like as not, and letting them all ride her."

I was about to protest—as if any of them dared or *could* ride Isabel—but instead, remembering in time, went on docilely with my supper. Outwardly impassive, I was sky-high within. Just as Isabel herself had always said, what a sensation to ride foaming up to school at a breakneck, hair-raising gallop. In the past I had indulged the prospect sparingly. Indeed, with so many threats and warnings in my ears, it had never been a prospect at all, but only a fantasy, something to be thought about wishfully, like blacking both Johnny Olsen's eyes at once, or having five dollars to spend. Now, though, everything was going to be different. Now, in their peculiar parental idiom, they had just given their permission, and Isabel and the future were all mine. Isabel *and* Millie Dickson. In accompaniment to a fervent resolve to be worthy of them both, my ears throbbed happily.

My
Uncle Joe

James McNamee

My uncle, Joe Campbell, said our family was Scotch. He should have said our family was almost Scotch, for my great-grandfather married a girl at Lac La Biche who was only half Scotch; her other half was Chipewyan Indian.

No matter how you look at it, Uncle Joe was one-eighth Chipewyan. I think this is why he always spoke kindly of poor Mr. Riel who was hanged. Mr. Riel was seven-eighths white and one-eighth Chipewyan.

I am one-sixteenth Chipewyan. I have enough Indian blood to make me a breed, but no darker than that other breed, the Englishman Winston Churchill, who is one-sixteenth Iroquois.

I was born Canadian, but my early years were spent at Fort Benton, Montana, where my father had six wagon outfits and three hundred mules. He hauled to the gold camps, and over the Whoop-Up Trail, and he had a trading post south of the Cypress Hills among the Sioux. My Uncle Joe worked for him. Joe rode around the country keeping an eye on things.

When I was twelve, in 1884, and I don't need you to tell me how old I am, my father asked himself, What is going to happen to me and my three hundred mules, the Northern Pacific Railway is building south of here and the Canadian Pacific has reached Medicine Hat, they will put Fort Benton and the Missouri River steamboats out of business, I am leaving.

He said to my uncle, We are moving back to Canada. There must be hauling to be done on the other side of the C.P.R. I want you to have a look, Joe. Take the buggy. No, take the buckboard and two spare horses. You can follow the Whoop-Up to Fort Macleod, then go to Fort Edmonton, then head east to Prince Albert, then down to Swift Current. That is a big hunk of country, Joe, and I want you to look it over well. Maybe you can find me some trading business with the Plain Crees or the Bush Crees, or among the Chipewyans, for we have relatives among the Chipewyans, Joe.

All right, my uncle said. When do I start?

This is September, Joe. You start right now. Come back in April or in May. Have a good look. And, Joe, I want you to take the boy.

You want me to do what! my uncle said.

I want you to take the boy, Joe.

Do I hear right? my uncle said. You want me to take the boy?

Yes.

Not in this life! my uncle said.

You listen to me, Joe. I want you to take the boy.

I am not taking the boy, my uncle said. He is a sick boy. I am not travelling among strange Indians I do not know if all the time I have to take my eyes off the country to wipe his nose.

Joe, my father said, the boy is pale, and he is small for his size, but he is not sick. He is only feeble. He has had the measles and the mumps, and now he has a cough. If we keep him inside he could get the sweating fever. He needs a lot of air. I have talked this over with his mother. It is all right, you can take him, for we have three other boys. Sleeping on the bald prairie may make him strong. Do not argue.

No! my uncle said.

Joe, who is boss here?

You are boss here.

Then you are taking the boy. Do not raise your voice at me. I have talked this over with his mother. And, Joe, on your way to Prince Albert I want you to stop among the French breeds at Batoche. My good friend, Mr. Riel, is at Batoche. He left St. Joseph's Mission here where he was teaching school. Give him a very big hello and my regards, for he is the one and only gentleman I ever met in Montana. Joe, do not argue. You are taking the boy.

We left Fort Benton in the buckboard on the fifth of September. It was one of those western days when the sun is the only thing not blue in all the sky.

My mother must have thought we were going to the North Pole. She had put so many clothes on me I was built up like an onion. I had a woollen cap with a green tassel that bumped against my cheek, and around my neck she had tied a woollen scarf. I wore red flannel underwear. I had beaded moccasins and woollen socks, buckskin pants, flannel shirt and a blue jersey, buckskin jacket, and a woollen overcoat that belonged to one of my big brothers. She didn't want me to catch cold. She told me of the pill I had to take in the morning and the syrup to take at night. She kissed me. She ran into the bedroom and I could hear her cry. I was twelve years old, but my father picked me up and carried me out of the house and put me in the buckboard. My father said, all right, okay, okay, get out of here, Joe. He put his hand in his pocket and he gave me a beautiful twenty-dollar gold piece. My brothers followed the buckboard for a quarter of a mile, yipping and yapping and hooting. When they stopped, they threw stones after us. That's the kind of brothers I had.

It was hot. I was sweating.

My uncle never said a word until we were crossing the Teton River. Then, when the water was so high I could reach down and touch it, he said, Whoa!

I thought he had decided that the river was getting too deep.

He said, We will have to go back to the house.

Why?

Because I see you are not wearing mitts. You must have forgotten them.

I said, They're in my pocket. Do you want me to put them on, Uncle Joe?

He did not answer. He flicked the horses with the buggy whip. I heard him say to himself, I can't make it out, I can't make it out, he does not behave like anybody on my side of the family.

I must have been a dumb kid.

We went another mile, then he said, Are you sure you are not cold? Would you like me to wrap you in one of the buffalo robes?

I said, I don't think so, uncle.

We went another mile. He said, Whoa!

Why are we stopping, uncle?

He said, Take the reins while I stand up and look behind.

What is it, uncle? Indians?

He said, I am not afraid of Indians. I am looking to see if I can see your mother. No, I do not see your mother. I will take a chance. Then he said, Get down on the ground. Get off that seat. I am not driving any longer with an Eskimo. Take off that hat with the green tassel. Take off that overcoat. Take off that scarf. Take off that buckskin jacket. Take off that sweater and that shirt. Take off that red flannel.

I'll be naked, uncle!

You can keep your pants, boy.

Uncle, I'll catch my death of cold!

You have your choice. Do you want to catch your death of cold, or do you want to catch a couple of cuts from this buggy whip?

I'll take my clothes off, uncle.

You do that, boy. You may be feeble in the head and in

other places, but if an Indian can do without a shirt in the month of October, you can do without a shirt in the month of September.

Right then and there I quit feeling like a delicate child. I never knew warm air could be so good. It made me think of Saturday night after I had had my bath and was standing in front of the coal-burner. Even the country seemed changed. Now it wasn't just grass and dirt. It looked as if Someone had said, The sky is my blue ceiling but, boy, I'll have a thousand different colours on the baseboard and the floor, here's yellow, bright yellow, and look, here's yellow like a crusty custard, and this stuff, grey, or is it olive, who cares, I'll splash it on, and this place here, I'll have it looking like the neck of a pigeon, now purple, I've got a gallon of purple, I've even got some of that crazy pinky-purple, and, well, well, what do you know, here's a can of good Irish green, this time of year we'll go easy on the green, how about red, you want red, okay, red for the red willow, there, that should be enough, now hand me the small brush and I'll put black on for the shadows in this coulee.

I threw all that wool I had been wearing in the back of the buckboard.

My uncle never asked how I was feeling until we got down to the Yeast Powder Flats.

I told him I felt fine.

He said, I am glad to hear that, because you look like an oyster on the half-shell. It will be getting cold soon. Maybe you had better put on a shirt.

The red flannel one, uncle?

I don't care, boy. You're free now. Put on what you want. When I took you from your mother I rescued you from slavery.

I put on my buckskin jacket.

If you live through the night, my uncle told me, I'll let you ride bare-back on one of the horses.

One of the horses in front, uncle, or one of the two horses tied behind?

I don't care, boy. Suit yourself.

Thank you, uncle. Look, there's a dead crow.

Can you shoot rabbits, boy?

No.

Can you clean a prairie chicken?

No. There's another dead crow.

Can you build a fire? Can you hobble a horse?

No.

Good heavens! my uncle said, what have I with me. Could you fry a piece of bacon?

There's another dead crow! And there's another dead crow! Look! There are three dead crows! We're passing all kinds of dead crows!

Whoa! my uncle said. He sniffed at the air like a ground-hog. Do you smell anything, boy?

No.

You soon will, my uncle said.

I asked him, Who killed the crows?

He said, Don't talk to me for a moment, boy. I know who killed the crows. And when I think of it, I get mad. And when I get mad, I use a lot of ugly words. He took his Winchester rifle out of its leather case, and opened and shut the breech to click a shell into the chamber.

I said, Indians? I was too dumb to feel nervous. I felt excited.

He said, Boy, I like Indians, and you should like Indians, for Indians and the cream of the Scottish Campbells are cousins. Take the reins. I think I'll hold the gun for a while. Let the horses walk.

In about ten minutes I said, I smell something.

How do you like it, boy?

I don't. It's rotten.

He said, I hope you're not going to throw up.

No, uncle.

He said, Well, if you feel like throwing up, jump. Boys who throw up in this buckboard are never seen again.

I kept swallowing and swallowing spit.

I'm almost glad you're going to see this, Uncle Joe said. You're old enough now to know what some men will do for a dollar.

We came to it. It was on my uncle's side. On the ground lay a dead, swollen beast that I took to be a deer, but my uncle told me it was an antelope. It was covered with flies. A hind leg was missing. And there was another dead thing. A dog. An Indian dog. I knew it was an Indian dog because even in death an Indian dog did not look like a white man's dog.

You've seen it, my uncle said. Drive on.

What killed the crows, uncle?

Poison, he said.

Poison?

Yes. Wolfers, he said. Drive on.

His lips were moving. I knew they did not move in prayer. He was thinking swear words, not letting them come out because of me. I had heard of wolfers, but I didn't know what was a wolfer. My brothers, when they got mad at each other, would say, You wolfer! or You low-down wolfer! or You low-down, no-good, sneaking wolfer!

Whoa! my uncle said.

The horses stopped.

He said, Why don't you keep your eyes open, boy?

They are open.

Then you need glasses. There's one of them. Look ahead.

We were in land so rough and broken that, even if we had wanted to, we couldn't have taken the buckboard off the trail. Above a roll, in tossing grass, two hundred yards in front, I saw a black hat.

He won't be alone, my uncle said. Wolfers never are.

To the left, I saw a blond head popping up and down. It had no hat.

They run in a pack, my uncle said. There must be more. Look behind you. I'll keep my eyes on these two.

I saw nothing behind. When I turned around again, four men were standing on the roll, spread out from each other. Only the man on the far left was armed. He had a long, clumsy rifle.

We'll let them come to us, my uncle said. He took out his handkerchief and wiped the sights of the Winchester.

They started walking. When they were a hundred yards away, they spread out a little more. The man with the rifle was the farthest from us. Even at that distance they looked dirty. I could see stains and patches and holes in their clothes.

My uncle took the six-shooter he carried under his jacket and slipped it into his half-boot. Well, well, he said, and he spoke as quietly as if we were in the parlour at home, Well, well, this is very interesting. Here we are out on the prairie with four horses, and there they are, four men out on the prairie with no horses. Everybody knows, boy, that a man on the prairie has to have a horse. This is very interesting.

The men were a hundred feet away, two on each side of the trail.

Don't be afraid, boy, Uncle Joe said. The horses won't run. They know what a shot sounds like.

The men were getting close. I could hear the swish of their legs through the grass.

Uncle Joe raised the Winchester. He raised it enough to be able to put it to his shoulder and go bang before you could even say the word bang.

The men stopped.

My uncle said, just as cool, You boys want something? I wish you could have heard him say it. You would have thought he was passing out ice-cream at a Sunday-school picnic.

Maybe they had never met a man like my uncle. They looked at each other with their eyebrows up.

How's the wolfing business, boys?

The wolfer farthest out was carrying his gun with the butt under his shoulder. He knew that if he tried to get it to his shoulder, my uncle would put a hole in his head.

They were filthy. They looked as if their clothes had been taken from the Fort Benton garbage dump. The shortest one wore a greasy black coat with big glass buttons. He used a piece of rope to keep his pants from falling. They had hair all over. Hair stuck out from their necks like horns. They had enough hair to stuff a potato sack. And their hats! They must have been eating beef stew out of their hats. The blond wolfer, the one without a hat, wore only a pair of tight blue pants and a heavy undershirt. He didn't have so much hair. His beard was still shaped as if, not too long before, it had been trimmed by a barber. The others had knives, but he had nothing.

After seeing these people, I made up my mind that if one of my big brothers called me a wolfer I would wham him. Wolfers shot antelopes or old horses and poisoned the meat. Wolves and coyotes would take bites from the dead animal and that was the end of them. The wolfer got their hides. A lot of Indian dogs were lost because of wolfers. Indians killed wolfers, but nobody cared. To decent white men a wolfer wasn't white. I will say no more than this about them, and you will please excuse me, they were crumbs, and they were bums, and they were first-class rotten stinkers.

My uncle looked at the wolfer farthest away, the one with the gun, and said, Am I to believe that none of you boys can talk?

The man talked. The kind of grin he had on his face was the kind you'd see on an alligator. Ho-ho! Ha-ha! he said, are we glad to see you. Ho-ho! We was hoping someone would come by. Is that your little boy, captain? Ho-ho! He's a fine little boy.

I was fine all right. Fine enough to know he was no good. I wouldn't have given that man a burnt match.

Now just a minute, my uncle said. You don't want to talk with a heavy rifle under your arm. I'll send this fine boy over to get it.

I can put it on the ground, colonel.

Of course you can. But you're not going to. Just give it to the boy slow-like.

Colonel, you wouldn't take my gun! You're a white man. There are Indians around.

My uncle said, Seven-eighths of the time I feel like a white man, but this is the one-eighth when I don't. I want your gun. He said to me, Get it.

He never asked me if I was afraid to get it. I was. I passed the short wolfer with the glass buttons on his coat. He had a twisted, broken nose. I was walking like I always do, but it seemed to take an hour to get where I was going.

The man with the gun was about six-feet one-inch tall, but he looked to me to be about nine-feet two-inches tall.

He said, Ho-ho! little boy, ho-ho! Are you going to grow up to be a fine man like the colonel? Ho-ho!

He gave me the shivers. If I had met him at Fort Benton, I would have crossed to the other side of the street. I cradled my arms and he laid the gun across them. I passed behind the man with the glass buttons. He never turned to look. He kept looking at my uncle.

My uncle said to me, Don't climb up on the buckboard with it. It's cocked, ready to fire. Reaching down, he eased the hammer forward. He said to the wolfer, Do you always walk the prairie with a cocked gun?

Was it cocked? I didn't know it was cocked, captain.

You're a liar, my uncle said, and I would tell you what kind of a liar you are too, if the boy wasn't here. You were waiting for the others to come close, then you were going to take a shot at me and let them finish the job with their knives.

Captain, we wouldn't do that!

You're a liar, my uncle said. You're after our horses.

Ah, captain, those are cruel words!

Where are your own horses?

The Indians got them, captain. They sneaked in at night. They got all of them, and they got two bales of fur, and two rifles.

And now, my uncle said, in their own sweet time they'll be coming after you.

We know that, colonel. We've been hiding for three days. We'll never make it without horses. We're scared to move out. And we're hungry.

I know where you can get some meat, my uncle said.

Where?

Half a mile behind, my uncle said, there's a dead antelope and a dead dog. Help yourself. Now we're driving through. Don't be foolish and try to stop us.

What's the world coming to! said the wolfer. There's no more charity!

A mule-train should pass this way tomorrow, my uncle said. Perhaps they will have a wagon full of charity. I'm out of it myself. Stand where you are. We're driving through.

Oh, the shame of it! the wolfer said. You pulling out like this! The shame of it! There's no more charity in all the world! Leaving us to the Indians! You're worse than that other bunch we met. They wouldn't even give us a pound of flour.

When was this? my uncle asked.

Oh, weeks ago. We had poisoned a lot of meat two days out of Fort Walsh.

Go on, my uncle said.

We were out of grub. We met a white man in a Red River cart. He had four breed outriders with him, and his wife and two babies.

Was this on the Fort Walsh Trail?

No. We were a hundred miles from any trail. The white man was ready to give us some grub, but the outriders wouldn't let him. They wanted to shoot us.

Who were these sensible outriders? my uncle asked.

The wolfer said, Charlie knew one of them.

Who's Charlie?

I am, said the blond man without a hat.

My uncle said, Where did you get the tight blue pants, Charlie? Don't tell me. I'll tell you. You're a deserter from the North West Mounted Police.

I had seen pants like that before. At Fort Benton there were always Canadians hanging around who had deserted from the Mounted Police.

That's right, the blond man said. I couldn't go through another winter at Fort Pitt. But take me back across the line. You'll get a reward. Turn me over to the Police. Do anything you want, just get me out of here.

Charlie, who was the outrider you knew?

Gabriel Dumont, Charlie said. He is a leader of the French breeds.

Gabriel! my uncle said, Gabriel Dumont! The great Gabriel who scared the Blackfeet, and now he comes riding through Blackfoot country with only three men! So it was Gabriel who came south to get him! Do you know who was riding in the Red River cart, Charlie? Mr. Riel.

Louis Riel? Charlie asked.

Charlie, I don't like the way you said his name. You must be from Ontario.

I am, from Toronto.

I never heard of it, Charlie. Well, good-bye, boys.

Take me with you, Charlie said. Please! Turn me in. You'll make fifty dollars. Don't leave me here!

Charlie, there's no room for you. You're a wolfer. Good-bye.

The shame of it! the wolfer who was farthest away cried. The shame of it! Is there no charity in all the world! You're leaving us to the Indians. And you've got my gun. The shame of it!

You'll find your gun a little way up the trail, my uncle said.

We're hungry, captain.

Eat antelope, my uncle said.

As we went by, Charlie stood stiff and saluted my uncle. He said, Sir, I hope I have the pleasure of meeting you again.

That's a small hope, Charlie, my uncle said. You have been killing Indian dogs, now Indians will try to kill you. That's a fair trade. But if we do meet again, the pleasure will be all yours, it won't be mine. Good-bye, boys.

When I looked back, they were walking in a cluster. I said, Do you think they are hungry, uncle?

Would you feed a wolfer, boy?

I don't know. I only know how I feel when I'm hungry.

Boy, do you like veal?

Not much.

Then when we stop to put down the gun, we'll leave that veal roast your mother gave us. I don't like veal at all. We'll let them have it.

That was my Uncle Joe. A big, soft-hearted westerner.

The Bully

Gregory Clark

Aubrey was his name. He could have been about eight or nine years of age. I was about seven.

He would lie in wait for me on my way to school. Four times every day. Being at that time a very small, measly little boy consisting largely of freckles, knuckles, knees and feet, I believed devoutly in the principle of non-resistance. Even before I started to school, I had learned I could not run fast enough to escape predators among my fellow-beings. Nor had I the weight, speed or courage to fight when overtaken.

Aubrey was a large, loose boy with sallow skin, pale eyes, a nasal voice and a frustrated character. Nobody loved him. The teachers didn't like him. He was avoided in the schoolyard. In the knots and squads of children going to and coming from school, Aubrey, large and louty for his age, was always mauling, pushing, shoving the smaller kids. The groups would either hurry to leave him behind or stop and wait for him to go on. Nobody, nobody loved him.

Then he found me. I fancy he lived two blocks closer to the school than I. He would wait for me just around a corner. He would lie in wait in side alleys, lanes, behind hedges. As Aubrey was large for his age, I was small for mine. I found difficulty joining the right gangs of children heading to or from school. I, like Aubrey, found myself often walking alone.

Aubrey would throw me down and kneel on me, his knees on my biceps. He would glare down at me out of his pale eyes with a look of triumph. He would pretend he was going to spit on me. He would grind his fist on my nose, not too heavy, but revelling in the imagined joy of punching somebody on the nose. It was inexpressible pleasure to him to have somebody at his mercy.

I tried starting to school late; lingering at school after dismissal. I tried going new ways, around strange blocks. No use. Aubrey got me. I had no protectors. My father was a fighting man, who would have laughed if I had revealed to him my terror. "Why," he would have cried gaily, "punch him in the nose!"

After about two years, Aubrey vanished. I suppose his family moved away. But as the years came and went, like ever-rising waves of the tide of life and experience, my memory kept Aubrey alive. As I grew, the memory of him grew. When I was fifteen, the hateful memory of Aubrey was my age too. When I was twenty, there in my life still lived the large, sallow, cruel figure of Aubrey. My hatred of him matured, became adult, took on the known shape of a presence.

In the Vimy battle, by 8:30 a.m., I was the only officer left in my company. I had started, three hours earlier, the baby lieutenant. Now I was alone with 200 men.

Orders came, now that we had reached the crest and the last final wonderful objective, that the R.C.R. having been held up at a semi-final objective, there was a gap on our left between us and the Princess Pats.

"You will take the necessary party," orders said, "and bomb across to meet a party from the Patricias, which will start from their flank at 9 a.m. You should attempt to meet their party half-way across."

"Who," I said to my sergeant, Charlie Windsor, "will I take with me?"

It was a pretty dreadful time. It was sleeting. The air shook with shell fire, whistled and spat with machine-gun fire; and without shape or form, random monsters fell around us, belching up gray earth, gray smoke, gray men.

"Me," answered Sgt. Windsor, "and five others."

We got the canvas buckets and filled them with bombs. Sgt. Windsor got a Lewis gun and five pans for it. At 9 a.m., peering across the grisly expanse toward where the Patricias should be, we saw, sure enough, a glimpse of furtive forms, half a dozen of them, bobbing, dodging, vanishing, reappearing. They were coming toward us.

"They've already started!" said Sgt. Windsor, hoisting the Lewis.

"Let's go," I croaked.

So, bobbing, dodging, vanishing, reappearing ourselves, we seven headed out to meet the Pats half-way. Down into shell craters, up over crater lips; down into the next craters, pools, mud; fresh hot holes, charred and new-burned, big holes, little holes, we slithered and slid and crouched. Two or three times, we had to cringe while German stick bombs whanged close; we lobbed ours back until we got silence. Two or three times, Sgt. Windsor had to slide the nozzle of the Lewis over the lip of craters and spray half a pan of fire into brush clumps. And once into a tree, half-way up, out of which a gray sack fell, heavily.

But each time up, we saw the Pats coming to us. And their bombs rang nearer, and ours rang nearer to them. We now could hear each other's shouts of encouragement and greeting.

"One more spurt!" I assured my crew.

The Pats squad was led by a long-geared, rangy man for whom I felt sorry each time I glimpsed him coming toward us. A pity all men can't be half-pints in war!

Our next plunge would be the last. We could hear the Pats only a few yards away.

Out over the lip I crouched and hurtled, feet first. Feet

first, I slid into a big crater; and over its lip skidded, feet first, the rangy, long-geared Pat.

You're right. It was Aubrey.

His pale eyes stared incredulous and triumphant down into mine. His sallow face split in a muddy grin.

"Don't I know you, sir?" he puffed.

"You sure should," I sighed struggling erect as possible and holding out my hand.

Hate dies funny.

The Shining Red Apple

Morley Callaghan

It was the look of longing on the boy's face that made Joe
Cosentino, dealer in fruits and vegetables, notice him. Joe
was sitting on his high stool at the end of the counter where
he sat every afternoon looking out of the window at the
bunches of bananas and the cauliflowers and the tomatoes
and apples piled outside on the street stand, and he was
watching to see that the kids on the way home from school
didn't touch any of the fruit.

This skinny little boy, who was wearing a red sweater and
blue overalls, stood near the end of the fruit stand where
there was a pyramid of big red apples. With his hands linked
loosely together in front of him, and his head, with the
straight, untidy brown hair that hung almost down to his
blue eyes, cocked over to one side, he stood looking with
longing at the apples. If he moved a little to the right, he
would be out of sight of the window, but even so if he
reached his hand out to take an apple, Joe, sitting at the end

of the counter and watching, would surely see the hand. The sleeves of Joe's khaki shirt were rolled up, and as he sat on his stool he folded his hairy forearms across his deep chest. There wasn't much business, there seemed to be a little less every day, and sitting there week after week, he grew a little fatter and a little slower and ever so much more meditative. The store was untidy, and the fruit and the vegetables no longer had the cool, fresh appearance they had in the stores of merchants who were prosperous.

If the kid, standing outside, had been a big, resolute-looking boy, Joe would have been alert and suspicious, but as it was, it was amusing to sit there and pretend he could feel the kid's longing for the apple growing stronger. As though making the first move in a game, Joe leaned forward suddenly, and the boy, lowering his head, shuffled a few feet away. Then Joe, whistling thinly, as if he hadn't noticed anything, got up and went out, took out his handkerchief, and started to polish a few of the apples on the pile. They were big, juicy-looking apples, a little over-ripe and going soft. He polished them till they gleamed and glistened in the sun. Then he said to the kid, ''Fine day, eh, son?''

''Yeah,'' the kid said timidly.

''You live around here?''

''No.''

''New around here, eh?'' Joe said.

The kid, nodding his head shyly, didn't offer to tell where he lived, so Joe, chuckling to himself, and feeling powerful because he knew so surely just what would happen, went back to the store and sat down on the stool.

At first the little kid, holding his hands behind his back now, shuffled away out of sight, but Joe knew he would go no farther than the end of the stand; he knew the kid would be there looking up and down the street furtively, stretching his hand out a little, then withdrawing it in fear before he touched an apple, and always staring, wanting the apple more and more.

Joe got up and yawned lazily, wetting his lips and rubbing his hand across them, and then he deliberately turned his back to the window. But at the moment when he was sure the kid would make up his mind and shoot out his hand, he swung around, and he was delighted to see how the child's hand, empty and faltering, was pulled back. "Ah, it goes just like a clock. I know just what he'll do," Joe thought. "He wants it, but he doesn't know how to take it because he's scared. Soon he wants it so much he'll have to take it. Then I catch him. That's the way it goes," and he grinned.

But in a little while Joe began to feel that maybe he was making it far too hard for the kid, as though the apples were something precious and untouchable. So, doing a thing he hardly ever did, he went out onto the street, and, paying no atttention to the kid, who had jumped away nervously, he mopped his shining forehead and wiped his red mouth and lazily picked up one of the apples from the top of the pile, as though all such luxuries of the world were within his reach. He munched it slowly with great relish, spitting out bits of red skin, and gnawing it down to the core. The kid must have been very hungry, for his mouth dropped open helplessly, and his blue eyes were innocent and hopeless.

After tossing the core in a wide arc far out on the street, where it lay in the sunlight and was attacked by two big flies, Joe started back into the store thinking, "Now for sure he'll grab one. He won't wait now. He can't." Yet to tantalize him, he didn't go right into the store; he turned at the door, looked up at the sky, as though expecting it to rain suddenly.

The frightened kid had really been ready to take an apple then. He had been so ready that he couldn't turn his head away, even though he knew Joe was watching him, for the apple seemed to belong to him now that he had made up his mind to take it and it was so close to him.

While Joe was grinning and feeling pleased with his cunning, his wife came in from the room at the back of the store. She was a black-haired woman, wide-hipped and slow-moving now, with tired brown eyes. When she stood beside her husband with her hands on her hips, she looked determined and sensible. "The baby's sleeping now, I think, Joe.

It's been pretty bad the way she's been going on."

"That's good," Joe said.

"She feels a lot better today."

"She's all right."

"I feel pretty tired. I think I'll lie down," she said, but she walked over to the window and looked out at the street.

Then she said sharply, "There's a kid out there near the apples. One's gone from the top."

"I sold it," Joe lied.

"Watch the kid," she said.

"O.K.," Joe said, and she went back to the bedroom.

Eagerly Joe looked again for the kid, who stood rooted there in spite of the hostile glance of the woman. "I guess he doesn't know how to do it," Joe thought. Yet the look of helpless longing was becoming so strong in the kid's face, so bold and unashamed, that it bothered Joe and made him irritable. He wanted to quarrel openly with the boy. "Look at the face on you. Look out, kid, you'll start and cry in a minute," he said to himself. "So you think you can have everything you want, do you?" The agony of wanting was so plain in the boy's face that Joe was indignant. "Who does the kid think he is?" he muttered.

In the room back of the store there was a faint whimpering and the sound of a baby stirring. "Look at that, son," Joe said to himself, as though still lecturing the kid. "It's a nice baby, but it's not a boy. See what I mean? If you go round with that look on your face when you want things and can't get them, people'll only laugh at you." As he spoke Joe grew restless and unhappy, and he looked helplessly around the untidy store, as if looking upon his own fate.

The kid on the sidewalk, who had shuffled away till he was out of sight, came edging back slowly. And Joe, getting excited, whispered, "Why doesn't he take it when he wants it so much? I couldn't catch him if he took it and ran," and he got up to be near the corner of the window, where he could see the boy's hand if it came reaching out. "Now. Right now," he muttered, really hoping it would happen.

Then he thought, "What's the matter with him?", for the kid was walking away, brushing by the fruit stand. One of his hands was swinging loose at his side. Then Joe realized that that swinging hand was to knock an apple off the pile and send it rolling along the sidewalk, and he got up eagerly and leaned forward with his head close to the window.

The kid, looking up warily, saw Joe's face and he grew frightened. His own face was full of terror. Ducking, he ran.

"Hey!" Joe yelled, running out to the sidewalk.

In a wild way the kid looked around, but he kept on running, his legs in the blue overalls pumping up and down.

Grabbing an apple and yelling, "Hey, hey, kid, you can have it!", Joe followed a few steps, but the kid wouldn't look back.

Joe stood on the sidewalk, an awful eagerness growing in him as he stared at the shiny red apple and wondered what would happen to the kid he was sure he would never see again.

Exiled

Shizuye Takashima

Vancouver, British Columbia
March 1942

Japan is at war with the United States, Great Britain and all
the Allied Countries, including Canada, the country of my
birth. My parents are Japanese, born in Japan, but they have
been Canadian citizens for many, many years, and have
become part of this young country. Now, overnight our
rights as Canadians are taken away. Mass evacuation for the
Japanese!

"All the Japanese," it is carefully explained to me, "whether
we were born in Tokyo or in Vancouver are to be moved to
distant places. Away from the west coast of British Columbia
— for security reasons."

We must all leave, my sister Yuki, my older brother David, my
parents, our relatives — all.

Reprinted from *A Child in Prison Camp* ©1971, Shizuye Takashima, published by Tundra Books of Montreal.

The older men are the first to go. The government feels that my father, or his friends, might sabotage the police and their buildings. Imagine! I couldn't believe such stories, but there is my father packing just his clothes in a small suitcase.

Yuki says, "They are going to the foothills of the Rockies, to Tête Jaune. No one's there, and I guess they feel father won't bomb the mountains."

The older people are very frightened. Mother is so upset; so are all her friends. I, being only eleven, seem to be on the outside.

One March day, we go to the station to see father board the train.

At the train station

An empty bottle is tossed in the air. I stand away, hold my mother's hand. Angry, dark curses, a scream. A train window is broken.

Most of the men have been drinking. An angry man is shouting. The men are dragged violently into the trains. Father can be seen. He is being pushed onto the train. He is on the steps, turns. His head is above the shouting crowd. I see his mouth opening; he shouts to his friends, waves his clenched fist. But the words are lost in all the noise. Mother holds my hand tightly.

A sharp police whistle blows. My blood stops. We see a uniformed Mounted Police drag an old man and hurl him into the train. More curses, threats. The old train bellows its starting sound. White, hellish smoke appears from the top of its head. It grunts, gives another shrill blast. Slowly, slowly, the engine comes to life. I watch from where we stand, fascinated. The huge, black, round, ugly wheels begin to move slowly, then faster, and faster. Finally, the engine, jet dark, rears its body and moves with a lurch. The remaining men rush toward the train, scramble quickly into the moving machine.

Men crowd at the windows. Father is still on the steps, he seems to be searching the crowd, finally sees us, waves. Mother does not move. Yuki and I wave. Most remain still. The dark, brown faces of the men become small. Some are still shouting. Yuki moves closer to mother.

The long, narrow, old train quickly picks up speed as it coils away along the tracks away from all of us who are left at the station.

Mother is silent. I look at her. I see tears are slowly falling. They remain on her cheeks. I turn away, look around. The women and the children stare at one another. Some women cry right out loud. A bent old woman breaks out into a Buddhist prayer, moves her orange beads in her wrinkled hands, prays aloud to her God. Mother and the other women bow their heads. The silent God seems so far away.

Summer 1942

From March to September, 1942, my mother, my sister Yuki and I are alone in Vancouver. David, our brother, is taken away, for he is over eighteen and in good health. It's hard for me to understand. Our David, who is so gentle, considered an enemy of his own country. I wondered what he thought as his time came to leave us. He spoke very little, but I do remember him saying, "In a way it's better we leave. I am fired from my job. The white people stare at me. The way things are, we'd starve to death!"

"You are lucky. You can still live in your house. And your children are older. They are a comfort." Her words trail off.

Now our house is empty. What we can sell, we do for very little money. Our radio, the police came and took away. Our cousins who have acres of berry farm had to leave everything. Trucks, tractors, land, it was all taken from them. They were moved with only a few days' notice to Vancouver.

Strange rumors are flying. We are not supposed to own anything! The government takes our home.

Mother does not know what to do now that father is not here and David too is taken. She does not speak very much; she is too worried how we are to eat with all her men gone. So finally, Yuki goes to work. She is sixteen; she becomes help for an elderly lady. She comes home once a week to be with us and seems so grown up.

I grow very close to my mother. Because we are alone, I often go to different places with her. Many Japanese families who were moved from the country towns such as Port Hammond and Steveston on the west coast of B.C., are now housed in the Exhibition grounds in Vancouver, waiting to be evacuated.

One very hot summer day mother and I visit a friend of hers who has been moved there.

A visit to the Exhibition grounds

The strong, summer July sun is over our heads as we near the familiar Exhibition grounds. But the scene is now quite different from the last time I saw it. The music, the roller-coasters, the hawkers with their bright balloons and sugar candy are not there. Instead, tension and crying children greet us as we approach the grounds. A strong odor hits us as we enter: the unmistakable foul smell of cattle, a mixture from their waste and sweat. The animals were removed, but their stink remains. It is very strong in the heat. I look at mother. She exclaims, "We are treated like animals!" I ask mother, "How can they sleep in such a stink?" She looks at me. "Thank our Lord, we don't have to live like them. So this is where they are. They used to house the domestic animals here. Such a karma!"

As we draw close to the concrete buildings, the stench becomes so powerful in the hot, humid heat, I want to turn and run. I gaze at my mother. She only quickens her steps. It seems as if we are visiting the hell-hole my Sunday school teacher spoke of with such earnestness.

White, thin sheets are strung up carelessly to block the view of prying eyes. Steel bunkbeds, a few metal chairs, suitcases, boxes, clothes hanging all over the place to dry in the hot sour air, greet our eyes. Mother sits on a chair, looks at her friend. Mrs. Abe sits on the bed, nursing her baby. The child, half-asleep, noisily sucks her breast. Mrs. Abe looks down at it, smiles, looks at mother and says, "The food is much better now. We complained every day, refused to eat one day. They take all our belongings, even our husbands, and house us like pigs, even try to feed us pigs' food!"

Mrs. Abe opens her heart to mother. I look around. The children's voices echo through the huge concrete buildings. Some of them are running around. The cement floor smells of strong chemical. I stare at the gray, stained floor. Mrs. Abe seeing this, says "They wash it every week with some cleaner. As if they cared whether we lived or died."

A curious head pokes in from the drawn, frail curtain. Mrs. Abe sees this, becomes angry. "Nosy bitch!" she says aloud. The dark head disappears. Mrs. Abe turns to me, glares into my eyes, forgetting for a moment that I do not live here, that I am still a child and am not responsible for her unhappiness. I begin to feel uncomfortable. I gently nudge my mother. She reads my sign, rises to take her leave, bowing, speaking words of encouragement. Mrs. Abe bows, thanks mother,

She bursts into tears. Her child awakens, startled; she begins to cry. Several heads appear from behind the curtains, eyes peer with curiosity. Mrs. Abe holds the child close to her and weeps into its small neck. I quietly walk away.

From the corner of my eye I can see sweaty children; they gape at me. They know I am from the outside. I pretend I do not see them, I quicken my steps, I am outside. Here the animal stench again overwhelms me. I turn. Mother is behind me. "You are rude to leave like that," she scolds. Her dark eyes search mine. I feel bad, I look down. The concrete ground seems to melt from the blazing heat. I curl my toes in my white, summer shoes. They are dusty from the walk. I look up, "I'm sorry. I couldn't help it. Her crying, and the smell . . ." Mother takes my hand and we begin to walk to the tram stop. "Someday, you'll understand. Mrs. Abe is much younger than me. She is new in this country, misses her family in Japan. You know she has only her husband."

All the way home in the noisy tram, mother says very little. I, happy to leave the smelly, unhappy grounds, daydream. I think of the film with Tyrone Power Yuki promised to take me to one day.

Vancouver
September 1942

Now we have curfew. All Japanese have to be indoors by ten P.M. The war with Japan is fierce. People in the streets look at us with anger. My sister Yuki has to quit her job. No reason is given by the elderly lady. We wait, mother, Yuki and I, for our notice to go to the camps. Already many families have left.

A night out

Yuki holds my hand, begins to run. "We have to hurry, Shichan. It's close to ten. Can you run a bit?" "I'll try," I say, but my limp makes it hard for me to keep up. Yuki slows down. I wish mother were with us. Everything seems so dark. An old man comes towards us, peers at us in the dim light. His small eyes narrow, he shouts, "Hey, you! Get off our streets!" He waves his thin arms, "I'll have the police after you." Yuki pulls my arm, ignoring him, and we run faster towards our house. The man screams after us.

Mother is at the door when we arrive. She looks worried, "You are late." She sees us panting. "Did you two have trouble?" She closes the door quickly. "You know I worry when you're late, Yuki." Yuki sits on a chair, looks at mother. "I'm sorry. The film was longer than I thought. It was so great we forgot about the curfew."

Mother pours Japanese green tea. It smells nice. I sit beside her and drink the hot tea. I look around. The rooms are bare. Boxes are piled for storage in the small room upstairs. Our suitcases are open, they are slowly being filled. We are leaving for camp next week.

A siren screams in the night. Air-raid practice. I go to the window. All our blinds are tightly drawn. I peek out, carefully lifting them. I see one by one the lights in the city vanish. Heavy darkness and quiet covers Vancouver. It looks weird. But the stars, high, high above, still sparkle, not caring, still beautiful and happy. I feel sad to be leaving the mountains, the lovely sea. I have grown with them always near me.

"Come away from the window, Shichan," mother's voice reaches me. I turn. I feel sadness come from her too. She has lived here for so long: "Over twenty-five years — hard to believe—I was a young girl, full of dreams. America! Canada! all sounded so magical in Japan. Remember, we had no radio in those days, so all our knowledge of this country came from books. My own mother had come to Canada long before other women. She was brave, not knowing the language, young, adventurous, a widow with three children.

She took your uncle Fujiwara with her. He was thirteen. I went to my grandmother's; my sister, to an aunt. It seems so long ago.''

Mother often talks of the past. Her life on the tiny island sounds lovely, for she had a happy childhood, so full of love. I go to her. I see her hands folded neatly on her lap. She always sits like this, very quiet, calm. Her warm eyes behind her round glasses are dark and not afraid.

An end to waiting

We have been waiting for months now. The Provincial Government keeps changing the dates of our evacuation, first from April, then from June, for different reasons: lack of trains, the camps are not ready. We are given another final notice. We dare not believe this is the one.

Mother is so anxious. She has just received a letter from father that he is leaving his camp with others; the families will be back together. I feel so happy. He writes that he is being moved to a new camp, smaller than others, but it is supposed to be located in one of the most beautiful spots in British Columbia. It's near a small village, 1800 feet above sea level. The Government wants the Japanese to build their own sanatorium for the T.B. patients. I hear there are many Japanese who have this disease, and the high altitude and dry air are supposed to be good for them. I feel secretly happy for I love the mountains. I shall miss the roaring sea, but we are to be near a lake. Yuki says, ''They decided all the male heads of families are to rejoin their wives, but not the single men.'' So, of course, David will remain in his camp, far away.

We rise early, very early, the morning we are to leave. The city still sleeps. The fresh autumn air feels nice. We have orders to be at the Exhibition grounds. The train will leave from there, not from the station where we said good-bye to father and to David. We wait for the train in small groups scattered alongside the track. There is no platform. It is September 16. School has started. I think of my school friends and wonder if I shall ever see them again. The familiar mountains, all purple and splendid, watch us from afar. The yellowy-orangy sun slowly appears. We have been standing for over an hour. The sun's warm rays reach us, touch a child still sleeping in its mother's arms, touch a tree, blades of grass. All seems magical. I study the thin yellow rays of the sun. I imagine a handsome prince will come and carry us all away in a shining, gold carriage with white horses. I daydream, and feel nice as long as I don't think about leaving this city where I was born.

The crisp air becomes warmer. I shift my feet, restless. Mother returns; she has been speaking to her friend, "Everyone says we will have to wait for hours." She bends, moves the bundles at our feet: food, clothes for the journey. I am excited. This is my first train ride! Yuki smiles, she too feels the excitement of our journey. Several children cry, weary of waiting. Their mothers' voices are heard, scolding.

Now the orange sun is far above our heads. I hear the twelve o'clock whistle blow from a nearby factory. Yuki asks me if I am tired. I nod, "I don't feel tired yet, but I'm getting hungry." We haven't eaten since six in the morning. Names are being called over the loudspeaker. One by one, families gather their belongings and move towards the train. Finally, ours is called. Yuki shouts, "That's us!" I shout, "Hooray!" I take a small bag; Yuki and mother, the larger ones and the suitcases. People stare as we walk towards the train. It is some distance away. I see the black, dull colored train. It looks quite old. Somehow I had expected a shiny new one. Yuki remarks, "I hope it moves. You never know with the government." Mother looks, smiles, "Never mind, as long as we get there. We aren't going on a vacation; we are being evacuated."

Bang . . . bang . . . psst . . . the old train gurgles, makes funny noises. I, seated by the window, feel the wheels move, stop, move, stop. Finally, I hear them begin to move in an even rhythm slowly.

I look out the dusty window. A number of people still wait their turn. We wave. Children run after the train. Gradually, it picks up speed. We pass the gray granaries, tall and thin against the blue Vancouver sky. The far mountains, tall pines, follow us for a long time, until finally they are gone.

Mother sits opposite; she has her eyes closed, her hands are on her lap. Yuki stares out the window. A woman across the aisle quietly dabs her tears with a white cloth. No one speaks.

Running Away from Home

Constance Beresford-Howe

The real surprise—to me anyway—was not really what I did, but how I felt afterwards. Shocked, of course. But not guilty. You might say, and be right, that the very least a woman can be is shocked when she walks out on a sick and blameless husband after forty years. But to feel no guilt at all — feel nothing, in fact, but simple relief and pleasure — that did seem odd, to say the least. How annoying for God (not to mention Adam), after all, if Eve had just walked out of Eden without waiting to be evicted, and left behind her pangs of guilt, as it were, with her leaf apron?

In any case, I just walked out. There was no quarrel with Burt. No crisis at all. The clock chimed nine-thirty. I laid down the breakfast tray carefully (an apple and a cup of cocoa) on the hall desk, and went to my room and packed. Not a word to anyone, even myself, by way of apology or excuse. Why? And why just then? Truly I'm not sure yet, although my name is Eva.

Our house was full of clocks rustling their self-importance and coughing delicately like people in church — they had something to do with it. So did my first old-age pension cheque, which had come the day before like a hint. But what chiefly stopped me was the cold white autumn light pouring through the landing window as I climbed up with the tray. It seemed to bleach the stairway into something like a high white cell. The night before on TV I'd seen cells like that in Viet Nam or somewhere, for political prisoners. You saw them crouched at the bottom of narrow cages, looking up at the light. I've never had a political conviction in my life, unless you count being bored by politics. But there I was just the same. Under bars.

Behind the bedroom door Burt gave his dry, irritable little cough. In a few minutes he would call me in a voice sharp and light with his morning pain. The cup of cocoa on the tray one minute steamed blandly and the next wobbled and slopped itself into the saucer. His mouth would press tight in disgust. "Can't you — " he would say, exasperated, "can't you — "

What I packed first (the whole thing took only ten minutes) was *Wuthering Heights* and a poetry anthology from my bedside shelf; but I didn't forget the grosser animal, and also took along my blood-pressure pills, glasses, hairbrush, and warm old-woman underpants. At the last minute I pulled out the plug of the little FM radio, Neil's birthday present, and tucked it under my arm.

And that was all. Out I went. There was a grey skin puckering on the cocoa as I passed it. On the stairs came his thin voice: "Eva!" I closed the front door on it.

No trouble finding a taxi on Monkland Avenue. Dry, grey October day, touch of frost. Nobody I recognized about. The only hard thing about the whole escape was getting all my possessions — radio, suitcase, and ample rump — crammed into the cab with any kind of dignity. The driver considerately pretended not to notice what a struggle this was. As soon as I got settled and found some breath, I paused to count my money. The pension cheque and fourteen eighty-nine in house money. Not much to kidnap yourself on, to be sure. But enough.

"Where to, lady?" the driver asked.

And of course it was then my legs began to shake. The shaking moved up clear through me, belly and bones. For a minute I thought it might turn into crying or being sick; then with cold hands at my mouth I was astonished to find it was laughter in there, shaking to get out. The driver waited without interest, bored eyes on the traffic.

"Well, you tell me," I said, pressing a Kleenex against my sense of irony. He gave me a wary glance then, and I blew my nose to stop the laughing. Disgraceful. Shocking way to behave, all round. And where to, lady? Where, indeed? I had not given that a single thought. Certainly I couldn't go to Neil and his bitchy elegance of a wife. Or to our few friends who weren't dead or living in Arizona; they would be embarrassed, or scandalized, or both. No; I'd go it alone, and the farther away I could make it, the better. But of course you can't get far on a total of ninety-two eighty-nine, and my own bank account was down to nearly zero after a new winter coat. A bus to somewhere? Or a hotel here for a day or two, until I could get myself organized?

No, because getting organized in a place like the Laurentien Hotel, say, with its Murray's food and rules on every door would simply mean going back.

"No," I said out loud and put away the Kleenex. The driver waited resignedly. "Just drive downtown, will you?" The engine gnashed its teeth and we shot forward. "Right downtown — somewhere near St. Lawrence Main." Because now that I was collecting my wits a bit, I realized someone from Notre Dame de Grace couldn't find a better place to hide than the other side of Montreal. I could find a room somewhere in the crowded French east end, and it would do perfectly. As for later on, and what to do then, I hadn't the least idea. I sat back on the cab's torn upholstery and we skimmed away through the neat, respectable rows of prosperous flats, full of decent women at their custodial jobs — wheeling babies, raking leaves, lugging bags of food. And I waited to feel guilty, properly horrified at what I was doing. Nothing at all stirred except a quite objective interest in what would happen next. Not to have the faintest idea what I might do—or become—was a peculiarly new and interesting experience, all by itself.

Of course it turned out that I'd forgotten all sorts of necessary things like toothpaste and extra shoes and my strong-willed girdle. Possibly I wasn't quite so cool and objective as I'd like to think. But I couldn't help admiring myself for doing anything so wicked. Not everyone could have done it, specially with my Anglican upbringing. How cross God must have been—if he kept track at all of such lapses as mine. And quite possibly he was the kind of person who did. Somebody like the chap that drove my taxi, with eyes like the dots on dice, disapproving of the whole cab-taking race, even though he couldn't exist without them.

No sleep at all last night, otherwise I'd never be speculating at this point on the nature of God. But it was far from unpleasant to lie awake thinking, even tingling with nervous fatigue, with my old friend the tension headache licking at my forehead, and counting over with real dismay how little was left of my cash. Because I felt excited as a girl, and happy enough to fly.

What a bit of luck to find this place, for one thing. Not more than two crow-miles from N.D.G., but a different world. You could immerse in it; become invisible. Rue de la Visitation, let me hide myself in thee.

In this district all the streets below Sherbrooke are narrow rows of senile, eccentric houses peering out of grimy dormer windows set high under fanciful mansard roofs. Iron lace and absurd crenellated towers crown them; they haven't been painted for at least a generation and couldn't care less. In every downstairs window sags a yellow sign: ''Appartements à louer.''

When I rang the bell nobody came but a marmalade cat jumping to the bow windowsill to peer out through a stiff net curtain. I was just about to turn away, shifting the radio awkwardly under one arm, when at last there was a long clatter of bolts, chains, keys, from inside, and the door opened a very small crack. Nobody could be seen in there at all, and when I pushed, the door jammed on a chain.

"What is it?" someone asked crossly in English with a pungent Scots accent.

I looked down for the source of the voice, and some four feet from ground level saw one beady eye gleaming. A powerful smell of soap came rushing out through the crack.

"You have a room to rent?" I asked.

"No," said the voice, and at once the eye disappeared.

"Wait — your sign says — "

"My son forgot to take it down. We've got no rooms."

But the eye had reappeared, and was taking note of my new coat — a Blin & Blin with a dark mink collar; it was clearly having second thoughts.

"Well — " she said cautiously, "there is that basement apartment vacant now . . . but you wouldn't want an apartment?"

As soon as I heard the word I knew that was exactly what I wanted. Apartness was just what I craved. Whatever this one was like, I wanted it. "Yes, I might. Can I see it?"

"Cost you fifty-five a month," she said dubiously. "Gas and light extra."

"Well . . . let me see it."

Very slowly she let the door off its tether and the soap smell jumped out on me like a dog. When I stepped into the hall and my eyes adjusted to the weak light, it emerged that Mrs. MacNab was only a bit over four feet tall and not, as I first thought, a tall woman on her knees. She had scraped-back thin grey hair and a fierce, sallow little face under it. Her breastless body was tightly aproned like a narrow package in clean print. The old linoleum of the hall and the long staircase rising behind her were still damp with scrubbing. A thicket of mops and brooms stood against the dark, stained wallpaper, and she heaved aside a big bucket of suds to let me move past.

"I'll 'ave to get the key," she said, and after a pause, as if afraid I might steal the bucket, rushed off to the back of the house. I was left for some minutes to enjoy a steel engraving

called "Out of the Deep" portraying a frantically busy ship-
wreck. Very suitable. Only a life-hater like Mrs. M. would
keep a place so clean.

"It's down here—there used to be a separate entrance at
the back, but it's been closed off years now, the door's
jammed, you're better off anyhow using the front door.
There's two rooms down here and bath, you're real private."

She unlocked a door behind the stairs and, turning on a
light so dim it barely stirred the dark, led me down a flight of
bare cellar steps to still another door opposite a large, muttering furnace. It was hard to see much, but it smelled dry
and not very dirty, and felt warm.

More unlocking revealed a big room with two high-set
basement windows at one end, and a quite stately fireplace
with pillared mantelpiece. Across the hall occupied by the
looming furnace was a tiny kitchen housing one crooked
table and a gas stove with taps and dainty bowed legs—quite
probably the first model ever made. Next door was a bathroom almost (but luckily not quite) wholly filled with a huge
tub on claws. I liked the place. I liked it at once and a lot.
Which is something of a confession, because if I hadn't been
by that time — nearly noon — really terribly tired, I would
never have considered living in such a hole. As it was,
though, my back was half broken from the suitcase, and my
pressure was up, everything throbbed. So I said, "I'll give you
fifty a month for it."

"There's water-tax extra, a dollar fifty a month," Mrs. M.
said at once. Of course she had no blood to have pressure
with. And so we agreed, and the place was mine.

Long, suspicious negotiations then to cash my cheque
and extort some change from it. Then a brief wrangle when I
discovered the gas stove had only one functioning burner.
But finally I was blissfully, blessedly alone. The place was my
empire. The door was locked. I kicked off my shoes and lay
right down in Blin & Blin on the degenerate sofa-bed and
closed my eyes. Everything throbbed for a long time. And
then I actually fell asleep.

An Ounce of Cure

Alice Munro

My parents didn't drink. They weren't rabid about it, and in fact I remember that when I signed the pledge in grade seven, with the rest of that superbly if impermanently indoctrinated class, my mother said, "It's just nonsense and fanaticism, children of that age." My father would drink a beer on a hot day, but my mother did not join him, and — whether accidentally or symbolically — this drink was always consumed *outside* the house. Most of the people we knew were the same way, in the small town where we lived. I ought not to say that it was this which got me into difficulties, because the difficulties I got into were a faithful expression of my own incommodious nature — the same nature that caused my mother to look at me, on any occasion which traditionally calls for feelings of pride and maternal accomplishment (my departure for my first formal dance, I mean, or my hellbent preparations for a descent on college) with an expression of brooding and fascinated despair, as if she could not possibly expect, did not ask, that it should go with me as it did with other girls; the dreamed-of spoils of daughters — orchids, nice boys, diamond rings — would be borne home in due course by the daughters of her friends, but not by me; all she could do was hope for a lesser rather than a greater disaster — an elopement, say, with a boy who could never earn his living, rather than an abduction into the White Slave trade.

But ignorance, my mother said, ignorance, or innocence if you like, is not always such a fine thing as people think and I am not sure it may not be dangerous for a girl like you; then she emphasized her point, as she had a habit of doing, with some quotation which had an innocent pomposity and odour of mothballs. I didn't even wince at it, knowing full well how it must have worked wonders with Mr. Berryman.

The evening I baby-sat for the Berrymans must have been in April. I had been in love all year, or at least since the first week in September, when a boy named Martin Collingwood had given me a surprised, appreciative, and rather ominously complacent smile in the school assembly. I never knew what surprised him; I was not looking like anybody but me; I had an old blouse on and my home-permanent had turned out badly. A few weeks after that he took me out for the first time, and kissed me on the dark side of the porch — also, I ought to say, on the mouth; I am sure it was the first time anybody had ever kissed me effectively, and I know that I did not wash my face that night or the next morning, in order to keep the imprint of those kisses intact. (I showed the most painful banality in the conduct of this whole affair, as you will see.) Two months, and a few amatory stages later, he dropped me. He had fallen for the girl who played opposite him in the Christmas production of *Pride and Prejudice*.

I said I was not going to have anything to do with that play, and I got another girl to work on Makeup in my place, but of course I went to it after all, and sat down in front with my girl friend Joyce, who pressed my hand when I was overcome with pain and delight at the sight of Mr. Darcy in the white breeches, silk waistcoat, and sideburns. It was surely seeing

Martin as Darcy that did for me; every girl is in love with Darcy anyway, and the part gave Martin an arrogance and male splendour in my eyes which made it impossible to remember that he was simply a high-school senior, passably good-looking and of medium intelligence (and with a reputation slightly tainted, at that, by such preferences as the Drama Club and the Cadet Band), who happened to be the first boy, the first really presentable boy, to take an interest in me. In the last act they gave him a chance to embrace Elizabeth (Mary Bishop, with a sallow complexion and no figure, but big vivacious eyes) and during this realistic encounter I dug my nails bitterly into Joyce's sympathetic palm.

That night was the beginning of months of real, if more or less self-inflicted, misery for me. Why is it a temptation to refer to this sort of thing lightly, with irony, with amazement even, at finding oneself involved with such preposterous emotions in the unaccountable past? That is what we are apt to do, speaking of love; with adolescent love, of course, it's practically obligatory; you would think we sat around, dull afternoons, amusing ourselves with these tidbit recollections of pain. But it really doesn't make me feel very gay — worse still, it doesn't really surprise me — to remember all the stupid, sad, half-ashamed things I did, that people in love always do. I hung around the places where he might be seen, and then pretended not to see him; I made absurdly roundabout approaches, in conversation, to the bitter pleasure of casually mentioning his name. I daydreamed endlessly; in fact if you want to put it mathematically, I spent perhaps ten times as many hours thinking about Martin Collingwood — yes, pining and weeping for him — as I ever spent with him; the idea of him dominated my mind relentlessly and, after a while, against my will. For if at first I had dramatized my feelings, the time came when I would have been glad to escape them; my well-worn daydreams had become depressing and not even temporarily consoling. As I worked my math problems I would torture myself, quite mechanically and helplessly, with an exact recollection of Martin kissing my throat. I had an exact recollection of *everything*. One night I had an impulse to swallow all the aspirins in the bathroom cabinet, but stopped after I had taken six.

My mother noticed that something was wrong and got me some iron pills. She said, "Are you sure everything is going all right at school?"*School!* When I told her that Martin and I had broken up, all she said was, "Well so much the better for that. I never saw a boy so stuck on himself." "Martin has enough conceit to sink a battleship," I said morosely and went upstairs and cried.

The night I went to the Berrymans' was a Saturday night. I baby-sat for them quite often on Saturday nights because they liked to drive over to Baileyville, a much bigger, livelier town about twenty miles away, and perhaps have supper and go to a show. They had been living in our town only two or three years — Mr. Berryman had been brought in as plant manager of the new door-factory — and they remained, I suppose by choice, on the fringes of its society; most of their friends were youngish couples like themselves, born in other places, who lived in new ranch-style houses on a hill outside town where we used to go tobogganing. This Saturday night they had two other couples in for drinks before they all drove over to Baileyville for the opening of a new supper-club; they were all rather festive. I sat in the kitchen and pretended to do Latin. Last night had been the Spring Dance at the High School. I had not gone, since the only boy who had asked me was Millerd Crompton, who asked so many girls that he was suspected of working his way through the whole class alphabetically. But the dance was held in the Armouries, which was only half a block away from our house; I had been able to see the boys in dark suits, the girls in long pale formals under their coats, passing gravely under the street-lights, stepping around the last patches of snow. I could even hear the music and I have not forgotten to this day that they played "Ballerina", and — oh, song of my aching heart — "Slow Boat to China". Joyce had phoned me up this morning and told me in her hushed way (we might have been discussing an incurable disease I had) that yes, M.C. *had* been there with M.B., and she had on a formal that must have been made out of somebody's old lace tablecloth, it just *hung*.

When the Berrymans and their friends had gone I went into the living room and read a magazine. I was mortally depressed. The big softly lit room, with its green and leaf-brown colours, made an uncluttered setting for the development of the emotions, such as you would get on a stage. At home the life of the emotions went on all right, but it always seemed to get buried under the piles of mending to be done, the ironing, the children's jigsaw puzzles and rock collections. It was the sort of house where people were always colliding with one another on the stairs and listening to hockey games and Superman on the radio.

I got up and found the Berrymans' "Danse Macabre" and put it on the record player and turned out the living-room lights. The curtains were only partly drawn. A street light shone obliquely on the windowpane, making a rectangle of thin dusty gold, in which the shadows of bare branches moved, caught in the huge sweet winds of spring. It was a mild black night when the last snow was melting. A year ago all this — the music, the wind and darkness, the shadows of the branches — would have given me tremendous happiness; when they did not do so now, but only called up tediously familiar, somehow humiliatingly personal thoughts, I gave up my soul for dead and walked into the kitchen and decided to get drunk.

No, it was not like that. I walked into the kitchen to look for a Coke or something in the refrigerator, and there on the front of the counter were three tall beautiful bottles, all about half full of gold. But even after I had looked at them and lifted them to feel their weight, I had not decided to get drunk; I had decided to have a drink.

Now here is where my ignorance, my disastrous innocence, comes in. It is true that I had seen the Berrymans and their friends drinking their highballs as casually as I would drink a Coke, but I did not apply this attitude to myself. No; I thought of hard liquor as something to be taken in extremities, and relied upon for extravagant results, one way or another. My approach could not have been less casual if I had been the Little Mermaid drinking the witch's crystal potion. Gravely, with a glance at my set face in the black window above the sink, I poured a little whisky from each of the bottles (I think now there were two brands of rye and an expensive Scotch) until I had my glass full. For I had never in my life seen anyone pour a drink and I had no idea that people frequently diluted their liquor with water, soda, et cetera, and I had seen that the glasses the Berrymans' guests were holding when I came through the living room were nearly full.

I drank it off as quickly as possible. I set the glass down and stood looking at my face in the window, half expecting to see it altered. My throat was burning, but I felt nothing else. It was very disappointing, when I had worked myself up to it. But I was not going to let it go at that. I poured another full glass, then filled each of the bottles with water to approximately the level I had seen when I came in. I drank the second glass only a little more slowly than the first. I put the empty glass down on the counter with care, perhaps feeling in my head a rustle of things to come, and went and sat down on a chair in the living room. I reached up and turned on a floor lamp beside the chair, and the room jumped on me.

When I say that I was expecting extravagant results I do not mean that I was expecting this. I had thought of some sweeping emotional change, an upsurge of gaiety and irresponsibility, a feeling of lawlessness and escape, accompanied by a little dizziness and perhaps a tendency to giggle out loud. I did not have in mind the ceiling spinning like a great plate somebody had thrown at me, nor the pale green blobs of the chairs swelling, converging, disintegrating, playing with me a game full of enormous senseless inanimate malice. My head sank back; I closed my eyes. And at once opened them, opened them wide, threw myself out of the chair and down the hall and reached — thank God, thank God — the Berrymans' bathroom, where I was sick everywhere, everywhere, and dropped like a stone.

From this point on I have no continuous picture of what happened; my memories of the next hour or two are split into vivid and improbable segments, with nothing but murk and uncertainty between. I do remember lying on the bathroom floor looking sideways at the little six-sided white tiles, which lay together in such an admirable and logical pattern, seeing them with the brief broken gratitude and sanity of one who has just been torn to pieces with vomiting. Then I remember sitting on the stool in front of the hall phone, asking weakly for Joyce's number. Joyce was not home. I was told by her mother (a rather rattlebrained woman, who didn't seem to notice a thing the matter — for which I felt weakly, mechanically grateful) that she was at Kay Stringer's house. I didn't know Kay's number so I just asked the operator; I felt I couldn't risk looking down at the telephone book.

Kay Stringer was not a friend of mine but a new friend of Joyce's. She had a vague reputation for wildness and a long switch of hair, very oddly, though naturally, coloured—from soap-yellow to caramel-brown. She knew a lot of boys more exciting than Martin Collingwood, boys who had quit school or been imported into town to play on the hockey team. She and Joyce rode around in these boys' cars, and sometimes went with them—having lied of course to their mothers—to the Gay-la dance hall on the highway north of town.

I got Joyce on the phone. She was very keyed-up, as she always was with boys around, and she hardly seemed to hear what I was saying.

"Oh, I can't tonight," she said. "Some kids are here. We're going to play cards. You know Bill Kline? He's here. Ross Armour— "

"I'm *sick*," I said, trying to speak distinctly; it came out an inhuman croak. "I'm *drunk*, Joyce!" Then I fell off the stool and the receiver dropped out of my hand and banged for a while dismally against the wall.

I had not told Joyce where I was, so after thinking about it for a moment she phoned my mother, and using the elaborate and unnecessary subterfuge that young girls delight in, she found out. She and Kay and the boys—there were three of them—told some story about where they were going to Kay's mother, and got into the car and drove out. They found me still lying on the broadloom carpet in the hall; I had been sick again, and this time I had not made it to the bathroom.

It turned out that Kay Stringer, who arrived on this scene only by accident, was exactly the person I needed. She loved a crisis, particularly one like this, which had a shady and scandalous aspect and which must be kept secret from the adult world. She became excited, aggressive, efficient; that energy which was termed wildness was simply the overflow of a great female instinct to manage, comfort and control. I could hear her voice coming at me from all directions, telling me not to worry, telling Joyce to find the biggest coffeepot they had and make it full of coffee (*strong* coffee, she said), telling the boys to pick me up and carry me to the sofa. Later, in the fog beyond my reach, she was calling for a scrubbrush.

Then I was lying on the sofa, covered with some kind of crocheted throw they had found in the bedroom. I didn't want to lift my head. The house was full of the smell of coffee. Joyce came in, looking very pale; she said that the Berryman kids had wakened up but she had given them a cookie and told them to go back to bed, it was all right; she hadn't let them out of their room and she didn't believe they'd remember. She said that she and Kay had cleaned up the bathroom and the hall though she was afraid there was still a spot on the rug. The coffee was ready. I didn't understand anything very well. The boys had turned on the radio and were going through the Berrymans' record collection; they had it out on the floor. I felt there was something odd about this but I could not think what it was.

Kay brought me a huge breakfast mug full of coffee.

"I don't know if I can," I said. "Thanks."

"Sit up," she said briskly, as if dealing with drunks was an everyday business for her so I had no need to feel myself important. (I met, and recognized, that tone of voice years later, in the maternity ward.) "Now drink," she said. I drank, and at the same time realized that I was wearing only my slip. Joyce and Kay had taken off my blouse and skirt. They had brushed off the skirt and washed out the blouse, since it was nylon; it was hanging in the bathroom. I pulled the throw up under my arms and Kay laughed. She got everybody coffee. Joyce brought in the coffeepot and on Kay's instructions she kept filling my cup whenever I drank from it. Somebody said to me with interest, "You must have really wanted to tie one on."

"No," I said rather sulkily, obediently drinking my coffee. "I only had two drinks."

Kay laughed, "Well it certainly gets to you, I'll say that. What time do you expect *they'll* be back?" she said.

"Late, after one I think."

"You should be all right by that time. Have some more coffee."

Kay and one of the boys began dancing to the radio. Kay danced very sexily, but her face had the gently superior and indulgent, rather cold look it had when she was lifting me up to drink the coffee. The boy was whispering to her and she was smiling, shaking her head. Joyce said she was hungry, and she went out to the kitchen to see what there was — potato chips or crackers, or something like that, that you could eat without making too noticeable a dint. Bill Kline came over and sat on the sofa beside me and patted my legs through the crocheted throw. He didn't say anything to me, just patted my legs and looked at me with what seemed to me a very stupid, half-sick, absurd and alarming expression. I felt very uncomfortable; I wondered how it had ever got around that Bill Kline was so good looking, with an expression like that. I moved my legs nervously and he gave me a look of contempt, not ceasing to pat me. Then I scrambled off the sofa, pulling the throw around me, with the idea of going to the bathroom to see if my blouse was dry. I lurched a little when I started to walk, and for some reason — probably to show Bill Kline that he had not panicked me—I immediately exaggerated this, and calling out, ''Watch me walk a straight line!'' I lurched and stumbled, to the accompaniment of everyone's laughter, towards the hall. I was standing in the archway between the hall and the living room when the knob of the front door turned with a small matter-of-fact click and everything became silent behind me except the radio of course; and the crocheted throw inspired by some delicate malice of its own slithered down around my feet, and there — oh, delicious moment in a well-organized farce — there stood the Berrymans, Mr. and Mrs., with expressions on their faces as appropriate to the occasion as any old-fashioned director of farces could wish. They must have been preparing those expressions, of course; they could not have produced them in the first moment of shock; with the noise we were making, they had no doubt heard us as soon as they got out of the car; for the same reason, we had not heard them. I don't think I ever knew what brought them home so early — a headache, an argument — and I was not really in a position to ask.

Mr. Berryman drove me home. I don't remember how I got into that car, or how I found my clothes and put them on, or what kind of a good night, if any, I said to Mrs. Berryman. I don't remember what happened to my friends, though I imagine they gathered up their coats and fled, covering up the ignominy of their departure with a mechanical roar of defiance. I remember Joyce with a box of crackers in her hand, saying that I had become terribly sick from eating — I think she said *sauerkraut* — for supper, and that I had called them for help. (When I asked her later what they made of this she said, ''It wasn't any use. You *reeked.''*) I remember also her saying, ''Oh, no, Mr. Berryman I beg of you, my mother is a terribly nervous person, I don't know what the shock might do to her. I will go down on my knees to you if you like but *you must not phone my mother.''* I have no picture of her down on her knees—and she would have done it in a minute — so it seems this threat was not carried out.

Mr. Berryman said to me, ''Well I guess you know your

behaviour tonight is a pretty serious thing." He made it sound as if I might be charged with criminal negligence or something worse. "It would be very wrong of me to overlook it," he said. I suppose that besides being angry and disgusted with *me*, he was worried about taking me home in this condition to my strait-laced parents, who could always say I got the liquor in his house. Plenty of Temperance people would think that enough to hold him responsible, and the town was full of Temperance people. Good relations with the town were very important to him from a business point of view.

"I have an idea it wasn't the first time," he said. "If it was the first time, would a girl be smart enough to fill three bottles up with water? No. Well, in this case, she *was* smart enough, but not smart enough to know I could spot it. What do you say to that?" I opened my mouth to answer, and although I was feeling quite sober the only sound that came out was a loud, desolate-sounding giggle. He stopped in front of our house. "Light's on," he said. "Now go in and tell your parents the straight truth. And if you don't, remember I will." He did not mention paying me for my baby-sitting services of the evening and the subject did not occur to me either.

I went into the house and tried to go straight upstairs but my mother called to me. She came into the front hall, where I had not turned on the light, and she must have smelled me at once for she ran forward with a cry of pure amazement, as if she had seen somebody falling, and caught me by the shoulders as I did indeed fall down against the banister, overwhelmed by my fantastic lucklessness, and I told her everything from the start, not omitting even the name of Martin Collingwood and my flirtation with the aspirin bottle, which was a mistake.

On Monday morning my mother took the bus over to Baileyville and found the liquor store and bought a bottle of Scotch whisky. Then she had to wait for a bus back, and she met some people she knew and she was not quite able to hide the bottle in her bag; she was furious with herself for not bringing a proper shopping bag. As soon as she got back she walked out to the Berrymans'; she had not even had lunch. Mr. Berryman had not gone back to the factory. My mother went in and had a talk with both of them and made an excellent impression and then Mr. Berryman drove her home. She talked to them in the forthright and unemotional way she had, which was always agreeably surprising to people prepared to deal with a mother, and she told them that although I seemed to do well enough at school I was extremely backward — or perhaps eccentric — in my emotional development. I imagine that this analysis of my behaviour was especially effective with Mrs. Berryman, a great reader of Child Guidance books. Relations between them warmed to the point where my mother brought up a specific instance of my difficulties, and disarmingly related the whole story of Martin Collingwood.

Within a few days it was all over town and the school that I had tried to commit suicide over Martin Collingwood. But it was already all over school and the town that the Berrymans had come home on Saturday night to find me drunk, staggering, wearing nothing but my slip, in a room with three boys, one of whom was Bill Kline. My mother had said that I was to pay for the bottle she had taken the Berrymans out of my baby-sitting earnings, but my clients melted away like the last April snow, and it would not be paid for yet if newcomers to town had not moved in across the street in July, and needed a baby-sitter before they talked to any of their neighbours.

My mother also said that it had been a great mistake to let me go out with boys and that I would not be going out again until well after my sixteenth birthday, if then. This did not prove to be a concrete hardship at all, because it was at least that long before anybody asked me. If you think that news of the Berrymans' adventure would put me in demand for whatever gambols and orgies were going on in and around that town, you could not be more mistaken. The extraordinary publicity which attended my first debauch may have made me seem marked for a special kind of ill luck, like the girl whose illegitimate baby turns out to be triplets: nobody wants to have anything to do with her. At any rate I had at the same time one of the most silent telephones and positively the most sinful reputation in the whole High School. I had to put up with this until the next fall, when a fat blonde girl in grade ten ran away with a married man and was picked up two months later, living in sin — though not with the same man — in the city of Sault Ste. Marie. Then everybody forgot about me.

But there was a positive, a splendidly unexpected, result of this affair; I got completely over Martin Collingwood. It was not only that he at once said, publicly, that he had always thought I was a nut; where he was concerned I had no pride, and my tender fancy could have found a way around that, a month, a week, before. What was it that brought me back into the world again? It was the terrible and fascinating reality of my disaster; it was *the way things happened*. Not that I enjoyed it; I was a self-conscious girl and I suffered a good deal from all this exposure. But the development of events on that Saturday night — that fascinated me; I felt that I had had a glimpse of the shameless, marvellous, shattering absurdity with which the plots of life, though not of fiction, are improvised. I could not take my eyes off it.

And of course Martin Collingwood wrote his Senior Matric that June and went away to the city to take a course at a school for Morticians, as I think it is called, and when he came back he went into his uncle's undertaking business. We lived in the same town and we would hear most things that happened to each other but I do not think we met face to face or saw one another, except at a distance, for years. I went to a shower for the girl he married, but then everybody went to everybody else's showers. No, I do not think I really saw him again until I came home after I had been married several years, to attend a relative's funeral. Then I saw him; not quite Mr. Darcy but still very nice-looking in those black clothes. And I saw him looking over at me with an expression as close to a reminiscent smile as the occasion would permit, and I knew that he had been surprised by a memory either of my devotion or my little buried catastrophe. I gave him a gentle uncomprehending look in return. I am a grown-up woman now; let him unbury his own catastrophes.

The
Wild Goose

Ernest Buckler

I've never stopped missing my brother Jeff.

I'm all right; and then I pick up the rake he mended so
perfectly for me where the handle went into the bow; or I
come across where he'd scratched the threshing count on
the barn door, with one of those clumsy fives of his in it; or
it's time for someone to make the first move for bed; or some
winter dusk when the sun's drawing water down beyond the
frozen marshes — do you know that time of day? It's as if
your heart slips into low gear.

(I'm glad Jeff can't hear me. But I don't know, maybe he
wouldn't think it sounded soft. Just because he never *said*
anything like that himself — you can't go by that.)

I always feel like telling something about him then. I don't
know, if I can tell something to show people what he was
really like it seems to help.

The wild goose flew over this evening. The sky was full of
grey clouds. It looked as if it was worried about something. I

could tell about Jeff and the wild goose. I never have.

It really started the afternoon before. We went hunting about four o'clock. I was fourteen and he was sixteen.

You'd never know we were brothers. You could tell exactly how he was going to look as a man, and I looked like a child that couldn't make up his mind *what* shape his face would take on later. He could lift me and my load (though he'd never once glance my way if I tackled anything beyond my strength — trying to lead a steer that was tough in the neck, or putting a cordwood butt on top of the pile, or anything). But I always seemed the older, somehow. He always seemed to — well, look up to me or something, it didn't matter how often I was mean to him.

I could draw the sprawling back field on a piece of paper and figure out the quickest way to mow it, by algebra; but when I took the machine out on the field itself I wouldn't know where to begin. Jeff could take one look at the field and know exactly where to make the first swath. That was the difference between us.

And I had a quick temper, and Jeff never lost his temper except when someone was mad at *me*.

I never saw him mad at me himself but that one day. The day was so still and the sun was so bright the leaves seemed to be breathing out kind of a yellow light before they fell to the ground. I always think there's something sort of lonesome about that, don't you?

I'm no kind of a hunter. You wouldn't think I was a country boy at all.

But Jeff was. He was a wonderful shot; and the minute he stepped into the woods there was a sort of brightness and a hush in his face together, I can't describe it. It wasn't that he liked the killing part. He seemed to have a funny kind of love and respect for whatever he hunted that I didn't have at all. If I don't see any game the first quarter mile I get to feel like I'm just walking around on a fool's errand, dragging a heavy gun along. But Jeff's spell never slacked off for a second.

You'd have to live in the country to know what hunting meant to anyone like Jeff. And to know how he rated with the grown-up men; here's just this kid, see, and he knows right where to find the game, no matter how scarce it is, and to bring it home.

Anyway, we'd hardly gone any distance at all — we were just rounding that bend in the log road where there's the bit of open swamp and then what's left of the old back orchard, before the woods start — when Jeff halted suddenly and grabbed my arm.

"What's the matter?" I said.

I guess I spoke louder than ordinary, because I was startled. I hadn't thought of having to be cautious so soon.

Jeff's gun went up, but he didn't have time for even a chance shot. There was a flash of the big buck's flag. He'd been standing under the farthest apple tree. Then in a single motion, like the ripple in a rope when you hold one end in your hand and whap the other against the ground, he disappeared into the thicket.

Deer will sometimes stand and watch you for minutes, still as stone. Stiller than thunder weather. Stiller than holding your breath. So still you can't believe it. They're cocked for running, but you get the feeling they weren't there before you saw them. Your eyes seem to have plucked them right out of the air. Their feet don't seem to quite rest on the ground.

But the second you speak, they're off. The human voice is like a trigger.

It would have been a sure shot for Jeff. There wasn't a twig between them. It would have been the biggest buck anyone had brought home that year. Even I felt that funny sag in the day that you get when game's been within your reach except for carelessness and now there's nothing. You just keep staring at the empty spot, as if you should have known that was the one place a deer would be.

Jeff turned to me. His eyes were so hot in his head I almost crouched.

"For God's sake," he said, "don't you know enough to keep your tongue still when you're huntin'?"

It was like a slap in the face.

The minute Jeff heard what he'd said the anger went out of him. But you'd have to live in the country to know what a funny feeling it left between us. For one hunter to tell another he'd spoiled a shot. It was as if you'd reminded someone to take off his cap inside the house.

I didn't say a word. Only in my mind. I seemed to hear my mind shouting, "You just wait. You'll see. I'll never . . . never . . . " Never what, I didn't know — but just that never, never again . . .

Jeff rumbled with a laugh, trying to put the whole thing behind us, as a joke.

"Well," he said, offhand like, "that one certainly moved fast didn't he? But we'll circle around. Maybe we'll ketch him in the choppin', what?"

I didn't say a word. I just broke down my gun and took out the cartridge, then and there. I put the cartridge into my windbreaker pocket and turned toward home.

"Ain't you comin'?" Jeff said.

"What d'ya *think*?" I said.

I glanced behind me when he'd gone on. I don't know, it always strikes me there's something sort of lonesome about seeing anyone walk away back-to. I almost changed my mind and ran and caught up with him.

But I didn't. I don't know why I could never smooth things over with Jeff right away when I knew he was sorry. I wanted to then, but I couldn't. I had to hang on to the hurt and keep it fresh. I hated what I was doing, but there it was.

It was pitch dark when Jeff got home that night, but he didn't have any deer.

I sort of kept him away from me all the next day. I hated myself for cutting off all his clumsy feelers to make up. ("What was the algebra question you showed the teacher how to do when you was only ten?") It always kind of gets me, seeing through what anyone is trying to do like that, when they don't know you can. But I couldn't help it.

(Once Jeff picked up about fifty bags of cider apples nights after school. The day he took them into town and sold them he bought every single one of us a present. I followed him to the barn that evening when he went to tend the horse. He didn't hear me coming. He was searching under the wagon seat and shaking out all the straw around the horse. He didn't want to tell me what he was looking for, but I made him. He'd lost a five dollar bill out of the money the man at the cider mill had given him. But he'd kept the loss to himself, not to spoil our presents. That's what he was like.)

It was just about dusk when Jeff rushed into the shop the day after I'd spoiled his shot at the deer. He almost never got so excited he forgot himself, like I did. But he was that way then.

"Git your gun, Kenny, quick," he said. "There's a flock o' *geese* lit on the marsh."

It would be hard to explain why that gave even me such a peculiar thrill. Wild geese had something — well, sort of mystic — about them.

When the geese flew south in the fall, high in the sky, people would run outdoors and watch them out of sight. And when they turned back to the house again they'd have kind of a funny feeling. The geese seemed to be about the most—distant, sort of—thing in the world. In every way. You couldn't picture them on the ground, like a normal bird. Years and years ago Steve Hammond had brought one down, and it was still the first thing anyone told about him to a stranger. People said, "He shot a wild goose once," in the same tone they'd say of some famous person they'd seen, "I was close enough to touch him."

I was almost as excited as Jeff. But I kept rounding up my armful, pretending the geese didn't matter much to me one way or the other.

"Never mind the *wood*," Jeff said. He raced into the house for his gun.

I piled up a full load before I went into the house and dropped it into the box. It must have almost killed him to wait for me. But he did.

"Come on. Come on," he urged, as we started down across the field. "And put in a ball cartridge. We'll never git near enough fer shot to carry."

I could see myself hitting that small a target with a ball cartridge! But I did as he said.

When we got to the railroad cut, we crawled on our bellies, so we could use the embankment the rails ran along as a blind. We peeked over it, and there they were.

They were almost the length of the marsh away, way down in that mucky spot where the men cut sods for the dike, but their great white breasts looked big as pennants. They had their long black necks stretched up absolutely straight and still, like charmed cobras. They must have seen us coming down across the field.

Jeff rested the barrel of his gun on a rail. I did the same with mine. But mine was shaking so it made a clatter and I raised it higher.

"I'll count five," Jeff whispered. "Then both fire at once."

I nodded and he began to count.

"One. Two. Three . . . "

I fired.

Jeff's shot came a split second afterward. He gave me a quick inquisitive glance, but he didn't say a word about me firing before the count was up.

He threw out his empty shell and loaded again. But the geese had already lifted, as if all at once some spring in the ground had shot them into the air. They veered out over the river.

All but one, that is. Its white breast was against the ground and we didn't see it in the blur of wings until its own wings gave one last flutter.

"We got one!" Jeff shouted. "Well, I'll be *damned*. We got one!"

He bounded down across the marsh. I came behind, walking.

When I got there he was stroking the goose's soft down almost tenderly. It was only a dead bird to me now, but to him it seemed like some sort of mystery made flesh and shape. There was hardly a mark on it. The bullet had gone through his neck, fair as a die.

Then Jeff made a funny face. He handed the goose to me. He was sort of grinning.

"Here," he said. "Carry her. She's yours. That was some shot, mister."

"Mine?" I said.

"Sure." He looked half sheepish. "I'm a hell of a hunter, I am. I had two ball cartridges in this here pocket, see, and two shot in this one." He put his hand into the first pocket and held out two ball cartridges in his palm. "I guess I got rattled and put the shot in my gun instidd o' the ball. You know how far shot'd carry. It was you that got him, no doubt about *that.*"

I carried the goose home.

It didn't mean much to me, but he didn't know that. He could only go by what it would have meant to him, if he'd been the one to carry it home. I knew what he was thinking. This would wipe out what I'd done yesterday. And the men wouldn't look at me now the way they looked at a bookworm but the way they looked at a hunter.

I'm glad that for once I had the decency to pretend I was as excited and proud as he'd thought I'd be. I'm glad I didn't say a word — not then — to let him know I saw through the trick.

For I knew it was a trick. I knew I hadn't shot the goose. While he was counting I'd felt that awful passion to wreck things which always got into me when I was still smarting over something. I had fired before he did, on purpose. Way over their heads, to scare them.

The day Jeff went away we sort of stuck around close to each other, but we couldn't seem to find anything to say.

I went out to the road to wait for the bus with him. Jeff had on his good clothes. They never looked right on him. When I dressed up I looked different, but Jeff never did. I don't know why, but every time I saw Jeff in his good clothes I felt sort of — well, like *defending* him or something.

The bus seemed to take a long time coming. He was going away in the army. He'd be with guys who were twice as much like him as I was, but just the same I knew he'd rather be with me than with them. I don't know, buses are such darned lonesome things, somehow.

When the bus was due, and I knew we only had left what

few minutes it might be late, I tried to think of something light to say, the way you're supposed to.

The only thing that came into my mind was that day with the goose. It was a funny thing to bring up all of a sudden. But now we were a couple of years older I thought I could make something out of it to amuse him. Besides, when someone's going away you have the feeling that you ought to get everything straight between you. You hardly ever can, but you get that feeling.

"You shot the goose that day," I said, "didn't you?"

He nodded.

I'd never have opened my fool mouth if I'd known what was going to happen then. I'd felt sort of still and bad, but I hadn't felt like crying. How was I to know that the minute I mentioned that day the whole thing would come back so darn plain? I'd have died rather than have Jeff see my face break up like that.

But on the other hand, I don't care how soft it sounds, I'm sort of glad I did, now. He didn't look embarrassed, to see me cry. He looked so darned surprised—and then all at once he looked happier than I believe I ever saw him.

That was Jeff. He'll never come back. I don't even know which Korean hill it was—the telegram didn't say. But when I tell anything about him like this I seem to feel that *somewhere* he's sort of, I don't know, half-smiling—like he used to when we had some secret between us we'd never even discussed. I feel that if I could just make him absolutely clear to everyone he wouldn't really be dead at all. Tonight when the geese flew over I wished I knew how to write a book about him.

The geese didn't light this time. They never have since that day. I don't know, I always think there's something lonesome about wild geese.

But I feel better now. Do you know how it is?

New
Frontiers

Survival Ship

Judith Merril

Half a million people actually made the round trip to Space Station One that day to watch the take-off in person. And back on Earth a hundred million video screens flashed the picture of Captain Melnick's gloved hand waving a dramatic farewell at the port, while the other hand slowly pressed down the lever that would fire the ship out beyond the orbit of the artificial satellite, past the Moon and the planets, into unknown space.

From Station One, Earth, and Moon, a hundred million winged wishes added their power to the surge of the jets, as a rising spiral of fire inside the greatest rocket tower ever built marked the departure of the thrice-blessed ship, *Survival*. In the great churches, from pole to pole, services were held all day, speeding the giant vessel on its way, calling on the aid of the Lord for the Twenty and Four who manned the ship.

At mountain-top telescopes a dozen cameras faithfully

transmitted the messages of great unblinking glass eyes. Small home sets and massive pulpit screens alike looked to the sky to follow the flare dimming in the distance, to watch the man-made star falling away.

Inside the great ship Melnick's hand left the firing lever, then began adjusting the chin rest and the earphones of the acceleration couch. The indicator dash-board, designed for prone eye level, leaped into focus. Securing the couch straps with the swift competence of habit, the captain intently watched the sweep of the big second hand around the take-off timer, aware at the same time that green lights were beginning to glow at the other end of the board. The indicator reached the first red mark.

"The show's over, everybody. We're in business!" The mike built into the chin rest carried the captain's taut voice all over the ship. "Report, all stations!"

"Number one, all secure!" Melnick mentally ticked off the first green light, glowing to prove the astrogator's couch was in use.

"Number two, all secure!"

"Number three ..." "Four ..." "Five." The rhythmic sing-song of pinpoint timing in take-off was second nature by now to the whole crew. One after another, the green lights glowed for safety, punctuating the litany, and the gong from the timer put a period neatly in place after the final "All secure!"

"Eight seconds to black out," the captain's voice warned. "Seven...six...stand by." The first wave of acceleration shock reeled into twenty-four helmet-sheathed heads on twenty-four individually designed head rests. "Five————" *It's got to work*, Melnick was thinking, fighting off unconsciousness with fierce intensity. "Four————" *It's got to ... got to ...* "Three ———— " *got to ... got to ...* "Two ———— " *got to ...*

At the space station, a half-million watchers were slowly cleared from the giant take-off platform. They filed in long orderly lines down the ramps to the interior, and waited there for the smaller Earth rockets that would take them home. Waiting, they were at once elated and disappointed. They had seen no more than could be seen at the same place on any other day. The entire rocket area had been fenced off, with a double cordon of guards to make sure that too-curious visitors stayed out of range. Official explanations mentioned the new engine, the new fuel, the danger of escaping gases — but nobody believed it. Every one of the half-million visitors knew what the mystery was; the crew, and nothing else. Giant video screens all over the platform gave the crowd details and close-ups, the same they would have seen had they stayed comfortably at home. They saw the captain's gloved hand, at the last, but not the captain's face.

There was muttering and complaining, but there was something else too. Each man, woman, and child who went to the station that day would be able to say, years later, ''I was there when the *Survival* took off. You never saw anything so big in your life.''

Because it wasn't just another planet hop. It wasn't just like the hundreds of other take-offs. It was the *Survival*, the greatest spaceship ever engineered. People didn't think of the *Survival* in terms of miles-per-second; they said, ''Sirius in fifteen years!''

From Sunday supplements to dignified periodicals, nearly every medium of communication on Earth had carried the story. Brightly colored graphs made visibly simple the natural balance of life forces in which plants and animals could maintain a permanently fresh atmosphere as well as a self-perpetuating food supply. Lecture demonstrations and video-casts showed how centrifugal force would replace gravity.

For months before take-off, the press and video followed the preparations with daily intimate accounts. The world over, people knew the nicknames of pigs, calves, chickens, and crew members—and even the proper botanical name of the latest minor masterpiece of the biochemists, a hybrid plant whose root, stems, leaves, buds, blossoms, and fruit were all edible, nourishing, and delicious, and which had the added advantage of being the thirstiest CO_2 drinker ever found.

The public knew the nicknames of the crew, and the proper name of the plant. But they never found out, not even the half million who went to the field to see for themselves, the real identity of the Twenty and Four who comprised the crew. They knew that thousands had applied; that it was necessary to be single, under twenty-five, and a graduate engineer in order to get as far as the physical exam; that the crew was mixed in sex, with the object of filling the specially equipped nursery and raising a second generation for the return trip, if, as was hoped, a lengthy stay on Sirius's planet proved possible. They knew, for that matter, all the small characteristics and personal idiosyncrasies of the crew members — what they ate, how they dressed, their favorite games, theaters, music, books, cigarettes, preachers, and political parties. There were only two things the public didn't know, and couldn't find out: the real names of the mysterious Twenty and Four, and the reason why those names were kept secret.

There were as many rumors as there were newsmen or radio reporters, of course. Hundreds of explanations were offered at one time or another. But still nobody knew — nobody except the half-hundred Very Important Persons who had planned the project, and the Twenty and Four themselves.

And now, as the pinpoint of light faded out of the screens of televisors all over Earth, the linear and rotary acceleration of the great ship began to adjust to the needs of the human body. "Gravity" in the living quarters gradually approached Earth-normal. Tortured bodies relaxed in the acceleration couches, where the straps had held them securely positioned through the initial stage, so as to keep the blood and guts where they belonged, and to prevent the stomach from following its natural tendency to emerge through the backbone. Finally, stunned brain cells awoke to the recognition that danger signals were no longer coming through from shocked, excited tissues.

Captain Melnick was the first to awake. The row of lights on the board still glowed green. Fumbling a little with the straps, Melnick watched tensely to see if the indicator lights were functioning properly, sighing with relief as the one at the head of the board went dead, operated automatically by the removal of body weight from the couch.

It was right—it was essential—for the captain to wake up first. If any of the men had showed superior recuperative powers, it could be bad. Melnick thought wearily of the years and years ahead during which this artificial dominance had to be maintained in defiance of all Earth conditioning. But of course it would not be that bad, really. The crew had been picked for ability to conform to the unusual circumstances; they were all without strong family ties or prejudices. Habit would establish the new castes soon enough, but the beginning was crucial. Survival was more than a matter of plant-animal balance and automatic gravity.

While the captain watched, another light went out, and then another. Officers, both of them. Good. Three more lights died out together. Then men were beginning to awaken, and it was reassuring to know that their own couch panels would show them that the officers had revived first. In any case, there was no more time for worrying. There were things to be done.

A detail was sent off immediately to attend to the animals, release them from the confinement of the specially prepared acceleration pens, and check them for any possible damage incurred in spite of precautions. The proportions of human, animal, and plant life had been worked out carefully beforehand for maximum efficiency and for comfort. Now that the trip had started, the miniature world had to maintain its status quo or perish.

As soon as enough of the crew were awake, Lieutenant Johnson, the third officer, took a group of eight out to make an inspection of the hydroponic tanks that lined the hull. Nobody expected much trouble here. Being at the outermost part of the ship, the plants were exposed to high "gravity". The outward pull exerted on them by rotation should have held their roots in place, even through the tearing backward thrust of the acceleration. But there was certain to be a large amount of minor damage, to stems and leaves and buds, and whatever there was would need immediate repair. In the ship's economy the plants had the most vital function of all — absorbing carbon dioxide from dead air already used by humans and animals, and deriving from it the nourishment that enabled their chlorophyll systems to release fresh oxygen for re-use in breathing.

There was a vast area to inspect. Row upon row of tanks marched solidly from stem to stern of the giant ship, all around the inner circumference of the hull. Johnson split the group of eight into four teams, each with a biochemist in charge to locate and make notes of the extent of the damage, and an unclassified man as helper, to do the actual dirty work, crawling out along the catwalks to mend each broken stalk.

Other squads were assigned to check the engines and control mechanisms, and the last two women to awake got stuck with the booby prize—first shift in the galley. Melnick squashed their immediate protests with a stern reminder that they had hardly earned the right to complain; but privately the captain was pleased at the way it had worked out. This first meal on board was going to have to be something of an occasion. A bit of ceremony always helped; and above all, social procedures would have to be established immediately. A speech was indicated — a speech Melnick did not want to have to make in the presence of all twenty-four crew members. As it worked out, the Four would almost certainly be kept busy longer than the others. If these women had not happened to wake up last . . .

The buzzing of the intercom broke into the captain's speculations. "Lieutenant Johnson reporting, sir." Behind the proper, crisp manner, the young lieutenant's voice was frightened. Johnson was third in command, supervising the inspection of the tanks.

"Having trouble down there?" Melnick was deliberately informal, knowing the men could hear over the intercom, and anxious to set up an immediate feeling of unity among the officers.

"One of the men complaining, sir." The young lieutenant sounded more confident already. "There seems to be some objection to the division of work."

Melnick thought it over quickly and decided against any more public discussion on the intercom. "Stand by. I'll be right down."

All over the ship airducts and companionways led from the inner-level living quarters "down" to the outer level of tanks; Melnick took the steps three at a time and reached the trouble zone within seconds after the conversation ended.

"Who's the troublemaker here?"

"Kennedy — on assignment with Petty Officer Giorgio for plant maintenance."

"You have a complaint?" Melnick asked the swarthy, dungareed man whose face bore a look of sullen dissatisfaction.

"Yeah." The man's voice was deliberately insolent. The others had never heard him speak that way before, and he seemed to gain confidence from the shocked surprise they displayed. "I thought I was supposed to be a pampered darling this trip. How come I do all the dirty work here, and Georgie gets to keep so clean?"

His humor was too heavy to be effective. "Captain's orders, that's why," Melnick snapped. "Everybody has to work double time till things are squared away. If you don't like the job here, I can fix you up fine in the brig. Don't worry about your soft quarters. You'll get 'em later and plenty of 'em. It's going to be a long trip, and don't forget it." The captain pointed significantly to the chronometer built into the overhead. "But it's not much longer to dinner. You'd better get back to work if you want to hit the chow while it's hot. Mess call in thirty minutes."

Melnick took a chance and turned abruptly away, terminating the interview. It worked. Sullen but defeated, Kennedy hoisted himself back up on the catwalk, and then began crawling out to the spot Giorgio pointed out. Not daring to express their relief, lieutenant and captain exchanged one swift look of triumph before Melnick walked wordlessly off.

In the big control room that would be mess hall, social hall, and general meeting place for all of them for fifteen years to come — or twice that time if Sirius's planet turned out to be uninhabitable — the captain waited for the crew members to finish their checkup assignments. Slowly they gathered in the lounge, ignoring the upholstered benches around the sides and the waiting table in the center, standing instead in small awkward groups. An undercurrent of excitement ran through them all, evoking deadly silences and erupting in bursts of too-noisy conversation, destroying the joint attempt at an illusion of nonchalance. They all knew — or hoped they knew — what the subject of the captain's first speech would be, and behind the façade of bronzed faces and trimly muscled bodies they were all curious, even a little afraid.

Finally there were twenty of them in the room, and the captain rose and rapped for order.

"I suppose," Melnick began, "you will all want to know our present position and the results of the checkup." Nineteen heads turned as one, startled and disappointed at the opening. "However," the captain continued, smiling at the change of expressions the single word brought, "I imagine you're all as hungry and — er — impatient as I am, so I shall put off the more routine portions of my report until our other comrades have joined us. There is only one matter which should properly be discussed immediately."

Everyone in the room was acutely conscious of the Four. They had all known, of course, how it would be. But on Earth there had always been other, ordinary men around to make them less aware of it. Now the general effort to maintain an air of artificial ease and disinterest was entirely abandoned as the captain plunged into the subject most on everyone's mind.

"Our ship is called the *Survival*. You all know why. Back on Earth, people think they know why too; they think it's be-

cause of our plants and artificial gravity, and the hundreds of
other engineering miracles that keep us going. Of course,
they also know that our crew is mixed, and that our population is therefore"— the captain paused, letting an anticipa-
tory titter circle the room — "is therefore by no means fixed.
What they don't know, naturally, is the division of sexes in
the crew.

"You're all aware of the reason for the secrecy. You know
that our organization is in direct opposition to the ethical
principles on which the peace was established after World
War IV. And you know how the planners of this trip had to
struggle with the authorities to get this project approved.
When consent was granted, finally, it was only because the
highest prelates clearly understood that the conditions of
our small universe were in every way different from those on
Earth — and that the division proposed was *necessary for
survival.*"

The captain paused, waiting for the last words to sink in,
and studying the attitudes of the group. Even now, after a
year's conditioning to counteract earthly mores, there were
some present who listened to this public discussion of dangerous and intimate matters with flushed faces and embarrassed smiles.

"You all realize, of course, that this consent was based,
finally, on the basic principle itself." Automatically, out of
long habit unbroken by that year's intensive training, the
captain made the sign of the olive branch. *"Survival of the
race is the first duty of every ethical man and woman."* The
command was intoned meaningfully, almost pontifically,
and brought its reward as confusion cleared from some of
the flushed faces. "What we are doing, our way of life now,
has the full approval of the authorities. We must never forget
that.

"On Earth, survival of the race is best served by the increasing strength of family ties. It was not thought wise to
endanger those ties by letting the general public become
aware of our — unorthodox — system here on board. A
general understanding, on Earth, of the true meaning of the

phrase, 'the Twenty and the Four', could only have aroused a furor of discussion and argument that would, in the end, have impeded survival both there and here.

"The knowledge that there are twenty of one sex on board, and only four of the other — that children will be born outside of normal family groups, and raised jointly—I need not tell you how disastrous that would have been." Melnick paused, raising a hand to dispel the muttering in the room.

"I wanted to let you know, before the Four arrive, that I have made some plans which I hope will carry us through the initial period in which difficulties might well arise. Later, when the groups of six—five of us, and one of them in each — have been assigned their permanent quarters, I think it will be possible, in fact necessary, to allow a greater amount of autonomy within those groups. But for the time being, I have arranged a — shall we call it dating schedule?" Again the captain paused, waiting for tension to relieve itself in laughter. "I have arranged dates for all of you with each of them during convenient free periods over the next month. Perhaps at the end of that time we will be able to choose groups; perhaps it will take longer. Maternity schedules, of course, will not be started until I am certain that the grouping is satisfactory to all. For the time being, remember this:

"We are not only more numerous than they, but we are stronger and, in our social placement here, more fortunate. We must become accustomed to the fact that they are our responsibility. It is because we are hardier, longer-lived, less susceptible to pain and illness, better able to withstand, mentally, the difficulties of a life of monotony, that we are placed as we are—and not alone because we are the bearers of children."

Over the sober silence of the crew, the captain's voice rang out. "Lieutenant Johnson," Melnick called to the golden-haired, sun-tanned woman near the door, "will you call the men in from the tank rooms now? They can finish their work after dinner."

A Queen
in Thebes

Margaret Laurence

Fear of a war was not what had taken them to the cottage in the mountains. Everyone had feared war for so long that it seemed it might never happen after all. Nerves cannot be kept on edge year in and year out without a boredom taking hold of the tension, calcifying it, ultimately making the possibility of devastation seem impossible in the face of the continuing realities—the newspapers delivered each day to the door, the passing of seasons, the favourite T.V. serials which would, everyone somehow felt, continue in spite of the fires of hell or the Day of Judgement. No, they had simply gone to the mountains because it would be good to get the baby out of the stifling city for the summer, into the cooler air and the quiet. It was a long way for her husband to drive for the weekends, but he said he did not mind, and later in the summer he would be getting his two weeks' holiday. Her husband had built the cottage the year they were married. It was only a shack, really, and it was not close to any settlement or town. They had to bring in all their supplies, and they decided to have the tinned goods sent in all at once, by truck, enough to last the summer, so her husband would not have to bother with much shopping when he came up on the weekends. Although it was isolated, it was a place they both loved. The lake was nearby, azure, and alive with fishes, and the pine and tamarack brushed their low-sweeping boughs against the windows as the night wind stirred them. Her husband spent a day in getting enough firewood for a week, making certain everything was all right.

"You don't mind being alone here with Rex?" he said. "If anything happens, you can always walk down the hill to Benson's Garage, and phone me."

She was afraid, but she did not say so. He went back to the city then. The day after he left, the sky turned to fire, as though the sun had exploded.

The city was a long way off, down on the plains, too far for the death to reach here, but she saw it like the disintegrating sun, the light like no other light, a dark illumination and not the health which we associate with light. Then the dust cloud formed like the shape of a giant and poisonous toadstool, and she knew the thing had come which everyone had feared. She herself had feared it until it no longer seemed real, and now it had come. She did not scream or cry, after the first unbelieving cry. She hid her eyes, lest the sight damage them. She ran into the cottage and sat quite still. It grew dark, and the baby was crying. She fed him, picking him up with small stiff movements of her hands. Then she put him into his bed and he went to sleep. She did not think at all of the cloud or the light or the death, or of how it would be this moment in what had been the city. She was waiting for her husband to arrive.

In the morning, she looked out and saw the sun rising. The fire of it glowed red and quiet in the sky. For an instant she gazed at it in panic. Then she drew the curtains across the windows so the light would not infect her or the baby. Everything was all right, she calmed herself. It was only that she had never been away from people before, although she was twenty years old. Either her family or her husband had always been with her. He will soon come, she told herself. She fed the baby. Then she took out her purse mirror and combed her hair, so she would look nice when her husband arrived.

She lived this way for some days, going outside the shack only at night. Then one morning she knew the sun did not threaten her. She walked out in the daylight, although she still could not look directly at the sun. When she looked beyond the forest, in the direction of the far-off city, she remembered the death. She ran back to the shack and took the baby in her arms. She rocked him there, and for the first time she cried and could not stop. She mourned wordlessly, and when her tears were done and the violence of the pain had momentarily spent itself, she thought of herself and the baby. She set out, carrying the child, to find people.

When she reached the foot of the mountain, she found no-one at Benson's Garage. The place had been deserted. The money was gone from the till, but otherwise everything had been left as it was. The people must have felt that they were not far enough away, thinking of the dust that could enter them in the air they breathed, rotting the blood and bone. They must have fled to some more distant and uncontaminated place. She wondered dully if they had found such a place, or if they had only run into other deaths, other polluted places, other cities shattered and lying like hulked shadows on the earth. She became afraid of the air now herself, and because she felt safer on the mountain, she wanted to start back. But she thought of the telephone, and an unreasoning hope possessed her. She was certain her husband was still somewhere and that she would be granted the miracle of his voice. She lifted the receiver and dialled. There was no response. She tried again and again, but there was no sound. She replaced the phone carefully, as though it mattered. Then she took the baby and began walking up the hill.

She knew she had to find people. In the days that followed, she walked long distances through the forest, marking her way so she would not get lost. She walked down the hill on every side, through the heavy bracken and the snarled bushes, until her legs and arms were bleeding with the small incisions of thorns and branches, and her arms ached with the fatigue of carrying the child, for she would not leave him alone in the shack. But in all her treks she found no-one. At night she did not cry. She lay sleepless, her eyes open, listening to owls and wind, trying to believe what had happened.

The leaves of the poplar were turning a clear yellow, and she knew it was autumn. She looked with sudden terror at the tins of food on the shelves, and saw they were almost gone. She picked berries and cooked them on the wood stove, wondering how long they would keep. She had fished only to provide her daily needs, but now she caught as many fish as she could. She slit and cleaned them, and laid them out in the sun to dry. One afternoon she found a black bear from the forest, feeding on the outspread fish. She had no gun. At that moment she was not afraid of the animal. She could think only of the sun-dried fish, hers, the food she had caught. She seized a stick and flew at the bear. The creature, taken by surprise, looked at her with shaggy menace. Then it lumbered off into the green ferns and the underbrush.

Each evening now, when the child was asleep, she lighted one of the remaining candles for only a few minutes and looked at herself in the mirror. She saw her long brownish blond hair and her thin tanned face and eyes she hardly knew as hers. Sometimes she wondered if her husband would recognize her when he arrived. Then she would remember, and would pick up the child and hold him tightly, and speak his name.

"Rex — it's all right. We're going to be all right."

The baby, wakened by her tears, would be frightened, and then she would be sufficiently occupied in quieting him. Sometimes, after she had looked in the mirror, she would not recall what had happened. She would go to bed comforted by the thought of her husband's arrival and would sleep without dreaming of the human shadows which she had

long ago heard were etched on stone, their grotesque im-
mortality.

Only when the first snow fell did she really believe that her
husband was dead. She wanted and needed to die then, too,
but she could not bring herself to kill her son and she could
not leave him alone, so she was condemned to life.

The winter went on and on, and she thought they would
not live until spring. The snow was banked high around the
shack, and in the forest the hollows were filled with white, a
trap to her unsure feet. She stumbled and fell, gathering
firewood, and her axe severed the leather of the old boots
which had been her husband's, cutting deeply into her
ankle. She bound the wound clumsily, not expecting it to
heal. It did heal, but the muscle had been affected and she
walked with difficulty for a long time. She and the child were
always cold and usually hungry. The thought uppermost in
her mind was that she had to keep the fire going. She became
obsessed with the gathering of wood, and would go out and
drag the spruce branches back, even when the pile of boughs
outside the shack was still high.

She prayed for help to come, but none came. Gradually
she stopped praying. She did not curse God, nor feel she had
been deserted by Him. She simply forgot. God seemed related to what had once been and was no more. The room in
her mind where the prayers had dwelt became vacant and
uninhabited.

The thing she loved was the sound of the child's voice.
What she missed most now was not her husband's protec-
tive presence, nor his warmth, but the sound of human
voices. The child was learning to talk, and soon they would
be able to speak together, as people do. This thought heart-
ened her.

When she looked in the mirror now, she saw how bony
and drawn her face had become, but the wide eyes were
harder than before, and an alertness lurked in them. Her
hearing was becoming keener. She could hear the deer that
approached the cabin at night, and she would look out at
them, but although she tried making traps, she caught only

an occasional jack-rabbit. Once, seeing the deer, their bodies heavy with meat, she took the axe and went out, ready to attempt them. But they were too quick and they vanished into the night forest where she dared not follow.

The dried fish were almost gone. She lived in a semiconscious state, drugged by exhaustion and hunger. Even her despair had lost its edge and was only a dulled apprehension of hopelessness. One day she threw the bones of a rabbit out into the snow, and for a moment sank down beside them, summoning strength to walk back into the cabin. A flock of sparrows landed on the snow beside her and began to explore the gnawed bones. She remembered dimly having once put out bread crumbs for the birds in winter. Delicately, hardly realizing she was doing it, her hands moved with a swiftness she had not known she possessed. She reached out and seized. When she drew back her hands, she had a live sparrow in each. She throttled them between thumb and forefinger, and began to tear off the feathers even before the small wings had stopped palpitating. Stolidly, feeling nothing, she cooked the birds and ate them. Then she vomited, and frightened the child with the way she cried afterwards. But the next time, when she caught birds and felt the life ebbing away between her fingers, she did not vomit or cry.

When the days began to lengthen, and spring came, she did not know whether it mattered that she and Rex were still alive. She moved only between one sunrise and the next. She could not think ahead. When the pain took possession of her heart, she still believed that she did not care whether they lived or died. Yet every day she gathered the firewood and foraged for some kind of food, and nothing was loathsome to her now, if her teeth and stomach could turn it into one more day of life.

She had kept only an approximate accounting of seasons, but one day she realized that Rex must be nearly six years old. She was much stronger than she had been—how weak and stupid she had been in the early days, after the Change

—but now the boy was almost as strong as she. He was better at trapping rabbits and birds, and when he went to the lake, he never came back without fish. He would lie for hours on the shore, watching where the fish surfaced and which reedy places in the shallows were most likely to contain them. His eyes were better than hers, and his ears, and he had discovered for himself how to walk through the forest noiselessly, without allowing the ferns and bracken to snap under his feet.

At first she had tried to teach him things from that other world—how to read and how to pray. But he only laughed, and after a while she laughed, too, seeing how little use it was to them. She taught him instead what she had learned here —always to keep the fire going, always to gather wood, how to uproot dandelions and how to find the giant slugs where they concealed themselves on the underside of fallen logs. Then, gradually and imperceptibly, the boy began to teach her.

He was standing in the doorway now, and across his shoulders was a young deer with its throat slit.

"Rex—where? How?" They did not speak together tenderly and at length, as she once had imagined they would. Their days were too driven by the immediate matters of food, and in the evenings they wanted only to sleep. They spoke briefly, abruptly, exchanging only what was necessary.

The boy grinned. "I ran after it, and then I used my knife. You never tried. Why?"

"I tried," she said. She turned away. The boy was laughing softly to himself as he took the animal outside and began to skin it. She looked out the doorway at him as he squatted beside the deer, his face frowning in concentration as he tried to decide how to do something he had not done before. He took the skin off badly, and grew furious, and hacked at the slain animal with his knife. They ate meat that night, though, and that was what counted. But for the first time she felt a fear not of the many things there were to fear outside, but of something inside the dwelling, something unknown. When the boy was sleeping, she took out her mirror and looked. *I am strong*, she thought. *We can live. I have made this possible.* But her own eyes seemed unfamiliar to her, and she looked at the image in the glass as though it were separate from herself.

The years were no longer years but seasons — the season of warmth and growth, when the green forest provided deer and the lake swarmed with fish; the season of coolness and ripening, when the berries reddened on the bushes; the season of snow and penetrating chill, when the greatest fear was that the fire might die. But when, after all the seasons of care, the fire did die, it happened in spring, when the melting snow drenched into the shack one night through the weakening timbers of the roof. She had left the iron lid off the old stove so it would draw better, for the wood was not quite dry. It was her fault that the fire died, and both of them knew it. Rex was almost as tall as she was, now, and he grasped her wrist in his intensely strong hand and led her to see.

"You have killed the fire. Now what will we do? You are stupid, stupid, stupid!"

She looked at his other hand, which was clenched, and wondered if she dared draw away from his grip. Then some deep pride straightened her. She pried at the noose-like fingers which held her wrist, and she used her fingernails like talons. He let go and gazed his rage at her. Then he dropped his eyes. He was not yet full grown.

"What will we do?" he repeated.

She saw then that he was waiting for her to tell him, and she laughed—but silently, for she could not risk his hearing. She put her hands gently on his shoulders and stroked the pliant sun-browned skin until he turned to her and put his head against her in a gesture of need and surrender. Then, quickly, he jerked away and stood facing her, his eyes bold and self-contained once more.

"I have tried to strike fire from stone," she said. "We must try again."

They did try, but the sparks were too light and fleeting, and the shreds of birch bark never caught fire. They ate their meat raw that summer, and when the evenings lengthened into the cool of autumn, they shivered under the deer hides that were their blankets.

Rex became ill on meat that had spoiled. They had both been sick before, many times, but never as badly as this. He vomited until his stomach was empty, and still he could not stop retching. She gave him water and sat beside him. There was nothing else she could do. The cabin was almost a wreck now, for although they had tried to repair it, they lacked sufficient tools, and Rex was not old enough yet to invent new and untried ways of building. They hardly moved outside for many days, and in this period the shack's mustiness and disrepair came to her consciousness as never before, and she looked with fear at the feeble timbers and the buckling walls, thinking of the winter. One night, when Rex's fever was at its height, and he lay silently, contracted with pain, she tried to think back to the distant times before the Change. She had forgotten her husband. But she remembered that some words used to be spoken, something powerful when everything else had failed.

"I should — pray," she said.

He opened his eyes. "Pray?"

She felt then, in some remote and dusty room of her mind, that she had not imparted to him something which was his due. There was always too much to do. She was too tired to talk much in the evenings.

"We used to speak of God," she said. "All life comes from God. Something great and powerful, greater than we are. When many people lived, they used to say these things."

The boy looked at her vacantly, not comprehending. Later, however, he asked her again, and she attempted once more to tell him.

"All life comes from God —— " but she no longer understood this very well herself and could not express it.

Gradually the illness left, and Rex grew strong again. One day he came back to the shack and told her he had found a cave in the side of a cliff.

"It will be better for the winter," he said.

She knew he was right. They moved everything they had, the knives and axe, the worn utensils, the tattered blankets, the deer hides. When she left the shack she cried, and the boy looked at her in astonishment.

Late that summer there was a severe storm, and the lightning descended to earth all around them, gashes of white light streaking the sky and tearing apart the darkness. She crouched on the cave floor and hid her eyes, as she always did in the presence of a sudden violence of light. Her fear was mingled with a sorrow whose roots she could no longer clearly trace. The boy knelt beside her and put his hands on her hair, and spoke to her, not roughly but quietly. He was afraid of the lightning, too, for he had learned her fear. But he was less afraid than she. He had no memory, not even her dim and confused ones, of any other life.

When the storm was over, they saw that the lightning had set the forest ablaze, a long way off, on the crest of the hill beyond their territory. The boy went off by himself. He was away for several days and nights, but when he returned he was carrying a smouldering pine torch. Their fire came to life again, and as it flared up in the circle of stones on the floor of the dark cave, the boy made an involuntary movement, as though compelled by something beyond his own decision. He raised his hands and bowed his head. Then, as though feeling that this was not enough, he knelt on the rock of the cave floor. He looked up and saw her standing immobile beside him, and his eyes became angry. With a sharp downward motion of his hand, he signalled what she was to do.

Slowly, doubtfully, and then as she stared at him at last unresisting, she went down onto her knees beside the circle of stones that contained the living fire. Together they knelt before the god.

One day she looked at Rex and saw he was much taller than she. He killed deer now mainly with his spear, and unless it was an exceptionally dry summer when the deer moved away in search of grazing, they were always well supplied with meat. The boy's hair grew down around his shoulders, but he lopped it off with his knife when it grew too long, for it got in his way when he was hunting. The hair was growing now on his face, but he did not bother to cut this. Age had no meaning for them, but she tried to count, as they counted the dried fish and strips of dried venison for the winter. The boy would be fifteen, perhaps, or sixteen.

She told him, without knowing in advance that she was going to say it, that the time had come for them to try once more to find the people. They thought of them as *The People*, those who perhaps lived somewhere beyond the mountain. She believed in their existence, but Rex believed only occasionally.

"There are no people," he said now.

"Yes," she said. "We must try."

"Why?" he asked.

She did not reply. She could only repeat the same words, over and over. "We must try." Rex shrugged.

"You go, then."

So she went alone, walking through the forest, descending into gullies where the loose shale slid under her feet, drinking face down from mountain streams, trapping squirrel and rabbit when she could. For many days and nights she travelled, but she did not find the people. Once she came to some dwellings, a few houses with weeds grown into the doorways, but they were deserted except for the mice and rats which eyed her, unblinking, from the corners of the dusty floors. Finally she knew she could not travel far enough. She was not any longer certain, herself, that the people really existed. She turned and started back.

When she reached the mountain once more, and entered the cave, Rex looked different, or else her time away from him had enabled her to see him differently.

"You are back," he said, with neither gladness nor regret.

But that evening in front of the fire, she saw he really had changed. He knelt as before, but more hastily, more casually, as though it were not quite so important as it had been. He saw her questioning eyes.

"I was wrong," he explained.

"Wrong?" she was bewildered.

He indicated the fire. "This one is small. There is — something else."

He did not say anything more. He turned away and went to sleep. He wakened her at dawn and told her to come outside the cave. He pointed to the sun, which was appearing now over the lake, a red globe in the pale sky of morning.

"Our fire comes from there. The voices told me when you were not here. I was alone, and I could hear them. They were waiting for you to go away. You do not hear the voices. Only I can hear them, when I am alone."

He spoke almost pityingly, and with a certainty she had not heard before. She wanted to cry out against what he said, but she did not know why, nor what she could say to him.

"Look —— " he said. "You look."

He knew she could not look directly at the sun. She feared, always, that the sight would damage her. The man grinned and turned his face to the sky.

"I can look," he said. "I can look at God. The fire comes from there. He does as He wishes. If He is pleased, then all things will go well. If He is angry, then we will suffer."

He went into the cave and brought forth the liver and heart of the deer he had killed the evening before. He laid these on a raised slab of stone. He brought a pine brand and made a fire underneath the entrails. Then he knelt, not as he had inside the cave, but prostrating himself, forehead to the earth in obeisance.

"Shall I kneel?" she asked him.

"Yes," he said. "But you are not to touch this stone and this fire and this meat. That is for me to do."

She obeyed. There was nothing else she could do. When he had gone to the lake to fish, she went to the corner of the cave where the cooking pots were piled. She had dug a niche into the rock, and here her secret possession lay. She took out the bundle of dried leaves, unfolded them carefully, and held the mirror in her hands. She looked into it for a long time. It calmed her, as though it were a focus for the scattered fragments of herself. Dream and daylight hovered in uncertain balance within her, always. Only when she looked in the mirror did she momentarily know she really existed.

"What is that?" The man's voice was harsh. She glanced up and quickly tried to conceal what she held in her hands. She had never allowed him to see her looking at herself. He had never seen a mirror. He had seen his own image in the quivering lakewater, but never the sharp, painful, and yet oddly reassuring picture she had of her own cruel and gentle eyes.

"It is nothing," she told him.

He took hold of her hand and forced it open. He looked at the shining object. His face was puzzled, but only for an instant. He glanced out the cave entrance to the sky and the mid-morning sun. Then he hurled the mirror from his hand, and it shattered against the rock of the cave walls. After that, he hit her, again and again and again.

"You are unclean!" he cried.

She knew then he was afraid of her, too. They were afraid of each other.

The seasons went by, and she kept no account of time. Generally she was content. She sat crosslegged now on the wide ledge outside the cave entrance. She was scraping a deer hide with the bone blade Rex had made. He had discovered, on one of his longer trips, a place where the people used to live and where pieces of iron lay rusting, and he had brought some back and fashioned spearheads and knives and an axe. But these were kept for his use, for he needed them more in hunting than she did in scraping the hides and making them into clothes. It was slow work, this, but she did not mind. The sun of late spring warmed her, and the raw trilling of frogs from the lake made her feel glad, for this was a good time of year, with hunger gone. The fish and game were plentiful, and the roots and leaves of the dandelions were succulent and tender.

The pointed shadow of the altar stone on the rock ledge told her that he would soon be back from the forest. She must prepare food, for he would be hungry when he returned. He did not like to be kept waiting. That was as it should be. A man was hungry after hunting.

But still she sat in the sunshine, drowsing over her work. Then the insinuating voice began, humming its tune inside her, and she blinked and shook her head as though to shake the whispered song away, for when it came to her she felt threatened and unsafe and she did not want to listen. Rex said the voices came only to him. But she heard this voice occasionally, unknown to him, in the deep quietness of the morning, when the birds were suddenly still, or in the wind that brushed through the forest at night. She did not recall when the voice had begun. She did not have a name for herself, as Rex did, and although it was enough to be what she was, in some way the voice was connected with the name she had once held, the name which had been shattered somewhere, some time, like lakewater when a stone is thrown into it. She never understood what the voice was saying to her, with its jingling music, a monotonous chanting from a long way off and yet close to her as her blood. The words, familiar in form but totally unfamiliar in meaning, were like the dry and twisted shells she found on the shore of the lake, objects that had once contained live creatures, but very long ago, so that no trace of flesh remained. The voice echoed again now, hurting and frightening her.

> *Lavender's blue, dilly dilly, lavender's green,*
> *When you are king, dilly dilly, I shall be queen.*

She half shut her eyes, and listened intently, but still she could not understand and could only feel troubled by something untouchable, some mystery that remained just beyond her grasp.

Then, inside the cave, one of the children began crying, and she went to give comfort.

Stranger in Taransay

Farley Mowat

The village of Taransay straggles along a bleak piece of craggy shore on the outer Hebrides — those high-domed sentinels that guard the Scottish mainland coast from the driving fury of the Western Ocean. The few strangers who visit Taransay remember the acrid smell of peat smoke on the windswept hills, the tang of the dark local ale, and the sibilant patter of the Gaelic tongue spoken by the shepherds and fishermen who gather during the long evenings under the smoke-stained ceiling of the Crofter's Dram.

It is the only public house for many miles, and it holds within its walls the beating heart of Taransay, together with many of its memories. Strange objects hang from the narrow ceiling beams or crowd the shelves behind the bar — remembrances of ancient wrecks, flotsam of the northern seas, the trivia of time. Amongst them is a collection of tiny figures delicately carved in white bone. These are ranged in the place of honour on a centre shelf where they catch the eye and stir the mind to wonderment. There are narwhals, long-beaked and leaping from an ivory sea; walrus thrusting tiny tusks through a miniature kayak; three polar bears snarling defiance at a human figure whose upraised arm holds a sliver of a spear; and a pack of arctic wolves poised in dreadful immobility over a slaughtered muskox.

There is an alien artistry about those carvings that never sprang from the imagination of an island shepherd, yet all were carved in Taransay. They are the work of a man named Malcolm Nakusiak who was a voyager out of time.

Nakusiak's odyssey began on a July day in the mid-1800s, under a basalt cliff in a fiord on the eastern shore of Baffin Island. To the score or so of people who lived there, it was known as *Auvektuk* — the Walrus Place. It had no name in our language for no white man had ever visited it although each year many of them, in stout wooden vessels, coasted the Baffin shores chasing the Bowhead whale.

These great whales were no part of men's lives at Auvektuk. For them walrus was the staff of life. Each summer when the ice of Davis Strait came driving south, the men of Auvektuk readied spears, harpoons and kayaks and went out into the crashing tumult of the Strait. On the grinding edges of the floes they stalked obese, ton-weight giants that were armoured with inch-thick hide, and armed with double tusks that could rend a kayak or a man.

Of all the Auvektuk hunters, few could surpass Nakusiak. Although not yet thirty years of age, his skill and daring had become legendary in his own time. Young women smiled at him with particular warmth for Eskimo women do not differ from their sisters the world over in admiring success. During the long winter nights Nakusiak was often the centre of a group of men who chanted the chorus as he sang his hunting songs. But Nakusiak had another skill. He was blessed with fingers that could imbue carvings made of bone and walrus ivory with the very stuff of life. Indeed, life was a full and swelling thing for Nakusiak until the July day when his pride betrayed him to the sea.

On that morning the waters of the Strait were ominously shrouded with white fog. The hunters had gathered on the shore, listening to the ludicrous fluting voices of the first walrus of the season talking together somewhere to seaward. The temptation to go after them was great, but the risk was greater. Heavy fog at that time of the year was the precursor of a westerly gale and for a kayaker to be caught in pack ice during an offshore storm was likely to be fatal. Keen as they were for walrus meat, courageous as they were, these men refused the challenge. All save one.

Gravely ignoring the caution of his fellows, Nakusiak chose to wager his strength — and his luck — against the imponderable odds of the veiled waters. The watchers on the shore saw his kayak fade into obscurity amongst the growling floes.

With visibility reduced to about the length of the kayak, Nakusiak had great difficulty locating the walrus. The heavy fog distorted their voices and confused the direction, yet he never lost track of them and, although he had already gone farther to seaward than he had intended, he still refused to give it up and turn for home. He was so tautly concerned with the hunt that he hardly noticed the rising keen of the west wind . . . .

Some days later, and nearly two hundred miles to the southeast, a Norwegian whaler was pounding her way southward through Davis Strait. The dirty, ice-scarred wooden ship was laden to her marks with oil and baleen. Her crewmen were driving her toward the hoped-for freedom of the open seas, all sails set and drawing taut in the brisk westerly that was the last vestige of a nor'west gale.

In the crow's nest the ice-watch swung his telescope, searching for leads. He glimpsed something on a distant floe off the port bow. Taking it to be a polar bear he bellowed a change of course to the helmsman on the poop. Men began to scurry across the decks, some running for guns while others climbed partway up the shrouds to better vantage points. The ship shouldered her way through the pack toward the object on the ice and the crew watched with heightened interest as it resolved itself into the shape of a man slumped on the crest of a pressure ridge.

The ship swung into the wind, sails slatting, as two seamen scampered across the moving ice, hoisted the limp body of Nakusiak in their arms and danced their way back from floe to floe, while a third man picked up the Eskimo's broken kayak and brought it to the ship as well.

The whalers were rough men, but a castaway is a castaway no matter what his race or colour. They gave Nakusiak schnapps, and when he was through choking they gave him hot food, and soon he began to recover from his ordeal on the drifting ice. All the same, his first hours aboard the ship were a time of bewilderment and unease. Although he had seen whaling ships in the distance, and had heard many barely credible stories from other Eskimos about the Kablunait — the Big Ears — who hunted the Bowhead, he had never before been on a ship or seen a white man with his own eyes.

He began to feel even more disturbed as the whaler bore steadily toward the southeast, completely out of sight of land, carrying him away from Auvektuk. He had been hoping the ship would come about and head north and west along the coast into the open water frequented by the Bowheads, but she failed to do so, and his efforts to make the Kablunait realize that he must go home availed him nothing. When the ship reached open water, rounded Kap Farvel at the south tip of Greenland and bore away almost due east, Nakusiak became frantic. Feverishly he began repairing his kayak with bits of wood and canvas given to him by the ship's carpenter, but he worked so obviously that he gave away his purpose. The newly patched kayak was taken from him and lashed firmly to the top of the after hatch where it was always under the eye of the helmsman and the officer on watch. The whalers acted as they did to save Nakusiak's life, for they believed he would surely perish if he put out into the wide ocean in such a tiny craft. Because he came of a race that accepted what could not be altered, Nakusiak ceased to contemplate escape. He had even begun to enjoy the voyage when the terrible winds of his own land caught up to him again.

The whaler was southeast of the Faeroe Islands when another ice-born nor'west gale struck her. She was a stout ship and she ran ably before it, rearing and plunging on the following seas. When some of her double-reefed sails began to blow out with the noise of cannon fire, her crew stripped her down to bare poles; and when the massive rollers threatened to poop her, they broke out precious cases of whale oil, smashed them open and let the oil run out of the scuppers to smother the pursuing graybeards.

She would have endured the storm had not her mainmast shrouds, worn thin by too many seasons in the ice, suddenly let go. They parted with a wicked snarl and in the same instant the mainmast snapped like a broken bone and thundered over the lee side. Tethered by a maze of lines, the broken spar acted like a sea anchor and the ship swung inexorably around into the trough . . . broached, and rolled half over.

There was no time to launch the whaleboats. The great seas tramped over them, snatching them away. There was barely time for Nakusiak to grab his knife, cut the kayak loose, and wriggle into the narrow cockpit before another giant comber thundered down upon the decks and everything vanished under a welter of water.

Washed clear, Nakusiak and the kayak hung poised for a moment on the back of a mountainous sea. The Eskimo held his breath as he slipped down a slope so steep it seemed to him it must lead to the very bowels of the ocean. But the kayak was almost weightless, and it refused to be engulfed by the sucking seas. Sometimes it seemed to leap free and, like a flying fish, be flung from crest to crest. Sometimes it flipped completely over; but when this happened, Nakusiak, hanging head down beneath the surface, was able to right his little vessel with the twisting double paddle. He had laced the sealskin skirt sewn to the cockpit coaming so tightly around his waist that no water could enter the vessel. Man and kayak were one indivisible whole. The crushing strength of the ocean could not prevail against them.

The bit of arctic flotsam, with its human heart, blew into the southeast for so long a time that Nakusiak's eyes blurred into sightlessness. His ears became impervious to the roar of water. His muscles cracked and twisted in agony. And then, as brutally as it had begun, the ordeal ended.

A mighty comber lifted the kayak in curling fingers and flung it high on the roaring shingle of a beach where it shattered like an egg. Although he was half stunned, Nakusiak managed to crawl clear and drag himself above the storm tide line.

Hours later he was awakened from the stupor of exhaustion by the cries of swooping, black-backed gulls. His vision had cleared, but his brain remained clouded by the strangeness of what lay around him. The great waves rolled in from the sounding sea but nowhere on their heaving surface was there the familiar glint of ice. Flocks of sea birds that were alien both in sound and form hung threateningly above him. A massive cliff of a dull red hue reared high above the narrow beach. In the crevices of the cliff outlandish flowers bloomed, and vivid green turf such as he had never seen before crested the distant headlands.

The headlands held his gaze for there was something on them which gave him a sense of the familiar. Surely, he thought, those white patches on the high green places must be scattered drifts of snow. He stared intently until fear shattered the illusion. The white things moved! They *lived!* And they were innumerable! Nakusiak scuttled up the beach to the shelter of a water-worn cave, his heart pounding. He knew only one white beast of comparable size — the arctic wolf — and he could not credit the existence of wolves in such numbers...if, indeed, the things he had seen were only wolves, and not something even worse.

For two days Nakusiak hardly dared to leave the cave. He satisfied his thirst with water dripping from the rocks, and tried to ease his hunger with oily tasting seaweed. By the third day he had become desperate enough to explore the cliff-locked beach close to his refuge. He had two urgent needs: food...and a weapon. He found a three-foot length of driftwood and a few minutes' work sufficed for him to lash his knife to it. Armed with this crude spear his courage began to return. He also found food of sorts; a handful of shellfish and some small fishes that had been trapped in a tidal pool. But there were not enough of these to more than take the edge off his growing hunger.

On the morning of the fourth day he made his choice. Whatever alien world this was that he had drifted to, he would no longer remain in hiding to endure starvation. He determined to leave the sterile little beach and chance whatever lay beyond the confining cliffs.

It was a long and arduous climb up the red rock wall and he was bone weary by the time he clawed his way over the grassy lip to sprawl, gasping for breath, on the soft turf. But his fatigue washed out of him instantly when, not more than a hundred paces away, he saw a vast assemblage of the mysterious white creatures. Nakusiak clutched the spear and his body became rigid.

The sheep, with the curiosity characteristic of members of their family, were intrigued by the fur-clad figure on the rim of the cliff. Slowly the flock approached, led by a big ram with black, spiralled horns. Some of the ewes shook their heads and bleated, and in this action the Eskimo saw the threat of a charge.

The sheep bleated in a rising chorus and shuffled a few feet closer.

Nakusiak reached his breaking point. He charged headlong into the white mob, screaming defiance as he came. The sheep stood stupidly for a moment, then wheeled and fled, but already he was among them, thrusting fiercely with his makeshift spear.

The startled flock streamed away leaving Nakusiak, shaking as with a fever, to stare down at the two animals he had killed. That they were mortal beings, not spirits, he could no longer doubt. Wild with relief he began to laugh, and as the sound of his shrill voice sent the remaining sheep scurrying even farther into the rolling distance, Nakusiak unbound his knife and was soon filling his starving belly with red meat — and finding it to his taste.

That strange scene under the pallid Hebridean sky had been witnessed by the gulls, the sheep ... and by one other. Atop a ridge a quarter mile inland a sharp-faced, tough-bodied man of middle age had seen the brief encounter. Angus Macrimmon had been idly cleaning the dottle from his pipe when his practised shepherds' glance had caught an unaccustomed movement from the flock. He looked up and his heavy brows drew together in surprise as he saw the sheep converging on a shapeless, unidentifiable figure lying at the edge of the cliff. Before Macrimmon could do more than get to his feet he saw the shape rise—squat, shaggy and alien — and fling itself screaming on the flock. Macrimmon saw the red glare of blood against white fleece and watched the killer rip open a dead sheep and begin to feed on the raw flesh.

The Hebrideans live close to the ancient world of their ancestors, and although there are kirks enough on the Islands, many beliefs linger on that owe nothing to the Christian faith. When Macrimmon watched the murder of his sheep, he was filled not only with anger but with dread, for he could not credit that the thing he saw was human.

Cursing himself for having left his dog at home, the shepherd went for help, running heavily toward the distant village. He was breathless by the time he reached it. Armed with whatever they could find, a dozen men were soon gathered together, calling their dogs about them. Two of them carried muzzle-loading shotguns while another carried a long-barrelled military musket.

The day was growing old when they set out across the moors, but the light was still clear. From afar the shepherds saw the white flecks that were the two dead sheep. Grouped close, they went forward cautiously until one of them raised an arm and pointed, and they all saw the shaggy thing that crouched beside one of the sheep.

They set the dogs on it.

Nakusiak had been so busy slicing up meat to sun-dry in the morning that he did not notice the approaching shepherds until the frenzied outcry of the dogs made him look up. He had never before seen dogs like these and he had no way of knowing that they were domestic beasts. He sprang to his feet and stood uncertainly, eyes searching for a place of refuge. Then his glance fell on the grim mob of approaching shepherds and he sensed their purpose as surely as a fox senses the purpose of the huntsmen.

Now the dogs were on him. The leader, a rangy black-and-brown collie, made a circling lunge at this strange-smelling, strangely clad figure standing bloody handed beside the torn carcasses. Nakusiak reacted with a two-handed swing of the spear-haft, striking the bitch so heavily on the side of her head that he broke her neck. There was a hubbub among the shepherds, then one of them dropped to his knee and raised the long musket.

The remaining dogs closed in again and Nakusiak backed to the very lip of the cliff, swinging the shaft to keep them off. He lifted his head to the shepherds and in an imploring voice cried out: "*Inukuala eshuinak!* It is a man who means no harm!"

For answer came the crash of the gun. The ball struck him in the left shoulder and the force of the blow spun him around so that he lost his balance. There was a shout from the shepherds and they rushed forward, but they were still a hundred yards away when Nakusiak stumbled over the cliff edge.

There was luck in the thing, for he only fell free a few feet before bringing up on a rocky knob. Scrabbling frantically with his right hand he managed to cling to the steep slope and slither another yard or so past a slight overhang until he could lie, trembling and spent, on a narrow ledge undercut into the wall of rock.

When the men joined the hysterical dogs peering over the cliff edge, there was nothing to be seen except the glitter of waves on the narrow beach far below and the flash of gulls disturbed from their resting places.

The shepherds were oddly silent. They were hearing again that despairing cry, instantly echoed by the shot. Whatever the true identity of the sheep killer might be, they knew in their hearts that he was human, and the knowledge did not sit easily with them.

They shifted uncomfortably until the man who had fired spoke up defiantly.

"Whatever 'twas, 'tis gone now surely," he said. "And 'tis as well, for look you at the way it tore the sheep and killed the dog!"

The others glanced at the dead dog and sheep, but they had nothing to say until Macrimmon spoke.

"Would it not be as well, do you think, to make a search of the beach?"

"Ach, man, don't be daft!" the gunner replied irritably. "'Twould be the devil's own job to gang down there ... and for what? If that thing was alive when it fell, then 'tis certain dead enough now. And if 'twas never alive at all ... " He let the sentence lie unfinished.

Calling the dogs the shepherds moved homeward over the darkening moors, and each one wrestled with his doubts in silence.

There was no policeman at Taransay, and no one offered to carry a message to the nearest constable across the mountains to distant Stornaway. Macrimmon put the feelings of all the men into words when he was being questioned about the event by his wife and daughters.

"What's done is done. There's no good to come from telling the wide world what's to be found on the moors, for they'd no believe it. Best let it be forgotten."

Yet Macrimmon himself could not forget. During the next two days and nights he found himself haunted by the memory of that alien voice. Up on the inland moors sloping to the mountain peaks, the wind seemed to echo it. The cry of the gulls seemed to echo it. It beat into the hard core of the man and would not be silenced and, in the end, it prevailed.

On the third morning he stood once more at the edge of the cliff ... and cursed himself for a fool. Nevertheless, that dour and weatherbeaten man carefully lowered himself over the cliff edge. His dog wheened unhappily but dared not follow as his master disappeared from view.

The tide was driving out and the shingle glistened wetly far below him, but the shepherd did not look down. He worked his way skilfully, for in his youth he had been a great one at finding and carrying off the eggs of the cliff-nesting gulls. However, he was no youth now and before he had descended halfway he was winded and his hands were cut and bruised. He found a sloping ledge that ran diagonally toward the beach and he was inching his way along it when he passed close to a late-nesting gannet. The huge bird flung herself outward, violently flailing the air. A wing struck sharply against Macrimmon's face and involuntarily he raised a hand to fend her off. In that instant the shale on which his feet were braced crumbled beneath him and he was falling away toward the waiting stones.

Unseen on the cliff top the dog sensed tragedy and howled.

The dog's howl awakened Nakusiak from fevered sleep in the protection of the little cave which had been his first sanctuary. Here, on a bed of seaweed, he lay waiting for his body to heal itself. His swollen shoulder throbbed almost unbearably but he stolidly endured, for it was in his nature to endure. All the same, as he waited for time to work for him, he was conscious that there was nothing ahead in this alien world but danger and ultimate destruction.

When the dog's howl woke him, Nakusiak shrank farther into the recesses of his cave. His good hand clutched the only weapon left to him ... a lump of barnacle-encrusted rock. He lifted it and held it poised as the rattle of falling stones mingled with a wailing human shout outside his cave.

His heart beat heavily in the silence that followed. It was a silence that reminded Nakusiak of how it is when an ermine has cornered a ground squirrel in a rock pile and waits unseen for the trapped beast to venture out. Nakusiak was aware of anger rising above his pain. Was he not *Inuk* — a Man — and was a man to be treated as a beast? He changed his grip on the rock, then, with a shout of defiance, stumbled out of his sanctuary into the morning light.

The sun momentarily blinded him and he stood tensely

waiting for the attack he was sure would come. There was no sound ... no motion. The glare eased and he stared about him. On a thick windrow of seaweed a few yards away he saw the body of a man lying face down, blood oozing from a rent in his scalp.

Nakusiak stared at this, his enemy, and his heart thudded furiously as the inert body seemed to stir, and mumbled sounds came from its mouth. In an instant Nakusiak was standing over the shepherd, the lump of rock raised high. Death hovered over Angus Macrimmon, and only a miracle could have averted it. A miracle took place. It was the miracle of pity.

Nakusiak slowly lowered his arm. He stood trembling, looking down at the wounded man and the trickle of blood from the deep wound. Then with his good arm Nakusiak gripped the shepherd, rolled him over, and laboriously dragged his enemy up the shingle to the shelter of the cave.

A search party found the dog on the cliff edge the next morning and guessed grimly at what had happened. But the searchers only guessed a part of it. When a couple of hours later six of them, all well armed, reached the beach in a fishing skiff, they were totally unprepared for what they found.

A thin curl of smoke led them directly to the cave. When they came to peer fearfully into the narrow cleft, guns at the ready, their faces showed such baffled incredulity at the scene before them that Macrimmon could not forbear smiling.

"Dinna be frighted, lads," he said from the seaweed mattress where he lay. "They's none here but us wild folk and we'll no eat you."

Inside the cave a small driftwood fire kindled by Nakusiak with Macrimmon's flint and steel burned smokily. The shepherd's head was bound with strips of his own shirt, but his bruised back with its broken ribs was covered with the fur parka that had been on the back of the sheep stealer not long since. Beside him, staring uneasily at the newcomers,

Nakusiak sat bare to the waist, hugging his wounded shoulder with his good arm.

The Eskimo glanced nervously from Macrimmon's smiling face to the blob of heads crammed into the cave entrance, then slowly he too began to smile. It was the inexpressibly relieved grin of one who has been lost in a frightful void and who has come back into the land of men.

For many days Nakusiak and Macrimmon lay in adjoining beds in the shepherd's cottage while their wounds healed. Macrimmon's wife and daughters gave the Eskimo care and compassion, for they acknowledged their debt to him. For his part, he entertained them with songs in Eskimo, at which the good wife muttered under her breath about "outlandish things", but smiled warmly at the stranger for all of that.

As he was accepted by the Macrimmons, so was he accepted by the rest of the villagers, for they were kindly people and they were also greatly relieved that they did not have to bear the sin of murder. Within a few weeks the Eskimo was being referred to with affection by all and sundry, as "the queer wee laddie who came out of the sea".

Nakusiak soon adjusted to the Hebridean way of life, having accepted the fact that he would never be able to return to his own land. He learned to speak the language, and he became a good shepherd, a superb hunter of sea fowl and grey seals, and a first-rate fisherman as well. Three years after his arrival at Taransay, he married Macrimmon's eldest daughter and started a family of his own, taking the Christian name of Malcolm, at the insistence of the young local clergyman who was one of those who particularly befriended him. During the long winter evenings he would join the other men at the Crofter's Dram and there, sitting before the open fire, would whittle his marvellous little carvings as a way of describing to his companions the life he had known in the distant land of the Innuit.

So Nakusiak, the man who had come so far in space and time from the Walrus Place to find a strange destiny in an alien world, lived out his life in Taransay. But it was no exile's life. Long before he died at the end of the century and was buried in the village churchyard, he had become one with the people of that place; and his memory remains a part of their memory still.

One summer afternoon in our time, a young man who is Nakusiak's great-grandson knelt to read the inscription written by the Eskimo's clergyman friend and carved into one of the twin stones that stand over the graves of Malcolm and his wife. There was pride in the young man's face and in the set of his shoulders as he read the words aloud:

Out of the sea from what lands none can tell,
This stranger came to Taransay to dwell.
Much was he loved who so well understood
How to return for evil a great good.

Akua Nuten

Yves Thériault

Kakatso, the Montagnais Indian, felt the gentle flow of the air and noticed that the wind came from the south. Then he touched the moving water in the stream to determine the temperature in the highlands. Since everything pointed to nice June weather, with mild sunshine and light winds, he decided to go to the highest peak of the reserve, as he had been planning to do for the past week. There the Montagnais lands bordered those of the Waswanipis.

There was no urgent reason for the trip. Nothing really pulled him there except the fact that he hadn't been for a long time; and he liked steep mountains and frothy, roaring streams.

Three days before he had explained his plan to his son, the thin Grand-Louis, who was well known to the white men of the North Shore. His son had guided many whites in the regions surrounding the Manicouagan and Bersimis rivers.

He had told him: "I plan to go way out, near the limits of the reserve."

This was clear enough, and Grand-Louis had simply nodded his head. Now he wouldn't worry, even if Kakatso disappeared for two months. He would know that his father was high in the hills, breathing the clean air and soaking up beautiful scenes to remember in future days.

Just past the main branch of the Manicouagan there is an enormous rock crowned by two pines and a fir tree which stand side by side like the fingers of a hand, the smallest on the left and the others reaching higher.

This point, which Kakatso could never forget, served as his signpost for every trail in the area; and other points would guide him north, west, or in any other direction. Kakatso, until his final breath, would easily find his way about there, guided only by the memory of a certain tree, the silhouette of the mountain outlined against the clear skies, the twisting of a river bed, or the slope of a hill.

In strange territory Kakatso would spend entire days precisely organizing his memories so that if he ever returned no trail there would be unknown to him.

Thus, knowing every winding path and every animal's accustomed lair, he could set out on his journey carrying only some salt, tea, and shells for his rifle. He could live by finding his subsistence in the earth itself and in nature's plenty.

Kakatso knew well what a man needed for total independence: a fish-hook wrapped in paper, a length of supple cord, a strong knife, waterproof boots, and a well-oiled rifle. With these things a man could know the great joy of not having to depend on anyone but himself, of wandering as he pleased one day after another, proud and superior, the owner of eternal lands that stretched beyond the horizon.

(To despise the reserve and those who belonged there. Not to have any allegiance except a respect for the water, the sky, and the winds. To be a man, but a man according to the Indian image and not that of the whites. The Indian image of a real man was ageless and changeless, a true image of man in the bosom of a wild and immense nature.)

Kakatso had a wife and a house and grown-up children whom he rarely saw. He really knew little about them. One daughter was a nurse in a white man's city, another had married a turncoat Montagnais who lived in Baie-Comeau and worked in the factories. A son studied far away, in Montreal, and Kakatso would probably never see him again. A son who would repudiate everything, would forget the proud Montagnais language and change his name to be accepted by the whites in spite of his dark skin and slitty eyes.

The other son, Grand-Louis...but this one was an exception. He had inherited Montagnais instincts. He often came down to the coast, at Godbout or Sept-Iles, or sometimes at Natashquan, because he was ambitious and wanted to earn money. But this did not cause him to scorn or detest the forest. He found a good life there. For Kakatso, it was enough that this child, unlike so many others, did not turn into a phony white man.

As for Kakatso's wife, she was still at home, receiving Kakatso on his many returns without emotion or gratitude. She had a roof over her head, warmth, and food. With skilled fingers she made caribou-skin jackets for the white man avid for the exotic. This small sideline liberated Kakatso from other obligations towards her. Soon after returning home, Kakatso always wanted to get away again. He was uncomfortable in these white men's houses that were too high, too solid, and too neatly organized for his taste.

So Kakatso lived his life in direct contact with the forest, and he nurtured life itself from the forest's plenty. Ten months of the year he roamed the forest trails, ten months he earned his subsistence from hunting, trapping, fishing, and smoking the caribou meat that he placed in caches for later use. With the fur pelts he met his own needs and those of the house on the reserve near the forest, although these needs were minimal because his wife was a good earner.

He climbed, then, towards the northern limits of the Montagnais lands on this June day, which was to bring calamity of which he was completely unaware.

Kakatso had heard of the terrible bomb. For twenty years he had heard talk of it, and the very existence of these horrendous machines was not unknown to him. But how was he to know the complex fabric of events happening in the world just then? He never read the newspapers and never really listened to the radio when he happened to spend some hours in a warm house. How could he conceive of total annihilation threatening the whole word? How could he feel all the world's people trembling?

In the forest's vast peace, Kakatso, knowing nature's strength, could easily believe that nothing and nobody could prevail against the mountains, the rivers, and the forest itself stretching out all across the land. Nothing could prevail against the earth, the unchangeable soil that regenerated itself year after year.

He travelled for five days. On the fifth evening it took Kakatso longer to fall asleep. Something was wrong. A silent anguish he did not understand was disturbing him.

He had lit his evening fire on a bluff covered with soft moss, one hundred feet above the lake. He slept there, rolled in his blanket in a deeply dark country interrupted only by the rays of the new moon.

Sleep was slow and when it came it did not bring peace. A jumble of snarling creatures and swarming, roaring masses invaded Kakatso's sleep. He turned over time and again, groaning restlessly. Suddenly he awoke and was surprised to see that the moon had gone down and the night's blackness was lit only by stars. Here, on the bluff, there was a bleak reflection from the sky, but the long valley and the lake remained dark. Exhausted by his throbbing dreams, Kakatso got up, stretched his legs and lit his pipe. On those rare occasions when his sleep was bad he had always managed to recover his tranquillity by smoking a bit, motionless in the night, listening to the forest sounds.

Suddenly the light came. For a single moment the southern and western horizons were illuminated by this immense bluish gleam that loomed up, lingered a moment, and then went out. The dark became even blacker and Kakatso muttered to himself. He wasn't afraid because fear had always been totally foreign to him. But what did this strange event mean? Was it the anger of some old mountain spirit?

All at once the gleam reappeared, this time even more

westerly. Weaker this time and less evident. Then the shadows again enveloped the land.

Kakatso no longer tried to sleep that night. He squatted, smoking his pipe and trying to find some explanation for these bluish gleams with his simple ideas, his straightforward logic and vivid memory.

When the dawn came the old Montagnais, the last of his people, the great Abenakis, carefully prepared his fire and boiled some water for his tea.

For some hours he didn't feel like moving. He no longer heard the inner voices calling him to the higher lands. He felt stuck there, incapable of going further until the tumult within him died down. What was there that he didn't know about his skies, he who had spent his whole life wandering in the woods and sleeping under the stars? The sky over his head was as familiar to him as the soil of the underbrush, the animal trails and the games of the trout in their streams. But never before had he seen such gleams and they disturbed him.

At eight o'clock the sun was slowly climbing into the sky, and Kakatso was still there.

At ten he moved to the shore to look at the water in the lake. He saw a minnow run and concluded that the lake had many fish. He then attached his fire cord to the hook tied with partridge feathers he had found in the branches of a wild hawthorn bush. He cast the fly with a deliberate, almost solemn movement and it jumped on the smooth water. After Kakatso cast three more times a fat trout swallowed the hook and he pulled him in gently, quite slowly, letting him fight as much as he wanted. The midday meal was in hand. The Montagnais, still in no great hurry to continue his trip, began to prepare his fish.

He was finishing when the far-away buzz of a plane shook him out of his reveries. Down there, over the mountains around the end of the lake, a plane was moving through the sky. This was a familiar sight to Kakatso because all this far country was visited only by planes that landed on the lakes. In this way the Indian had come to know the white man. This was the most frequent place of contact between the two: a large body of quiet water where a plane would land, where the whites would ask for help and find nothing better than an Indian to help them.

Even from a distance Kakatso recognized the type of plane. It was a single-engine, deluxe Bonanza, a type often used by the Americans who came to fish for their salmon in our rivers.

The plane circled the lake and flew over the bluff where Kakatso's fire was still burning. Then it landed gently, almost tenderly. The still waters were only lightly ruffled and quickly returned to their mirror smoothness. The plane slowed down, the motor coughed once or twice, then the craft made a complete turn and headed for the beach.

Kakatso, with one hand shading his eyes, watched the landing, motionless.

When the plane was finally still and the tips of its pontoons were pulled up on the sandy beach, two men, a young woman, and a twelve-year-old boy got out.

One of the men was massive. He towered a head over Kakatso although the Montagnais himself was rather tall.

"Are you an Indian?" the man asked suddenly.

Kakatso nodded slowly and blinked his eyes once.

"Good, I'm glad, you can save us," said the man.

"Save you?" said Kakatso. "Save you from what?"

"Never mind," said the woman, "that's our business."

Standing some distance away, she gestured to the big man who had first spoken to Kakatso.

"If you're trying to escape the police," said Kakatso, "I can't do anything for you."

"It has nothing to do with the police," said the other man who had not spoken previously.

He moved towards Kakatso and proffered a handshake. Now that he was close the Montagnais recognized a veteran bush pilot. His experience could be seen in his eyes, in the squint of his eyelids, and in the way he treated an Indian as an equal.

"I am Bob Ledoux," the man said. "I am a pilot. Do you know what nuclear war is?"

"Yes," answered Kakatso, "I know."

"All the cities in the south have been destroyed," said Ledoux. "We were able to escape."

"Is that a real one?" asked the boy, who had been closely scrutinizing Kakatso. "Eh, Mom, is it really one of those savages?"

"Yes," answered the woman, "certainly." And to Kakatso she said, "Please excuse him. He has never been on the North Shore."

Naturally Kakatso did not like to be considered a savage. But he didn't show anything and he swallowed his bitterness.

"So," said the pilot, "Here we are without resources."

"I have money," said the man.

"This is Mr. Perron," said the pilot, "Mrs. Perron, and their son...."

"My name is Roger," said the boy. "I know how to swim."

The Montagnais was still undecided. He did not trust intruders. He preferred, in his simple soul, to choose his own objectives and decide his day's activities. And here were outsiders who had fallen from the sky, almost demanding his help...but what help?

"I can't do much for you," he said after a while.

"I have money," the man repeated.

Kakatso shrugged. Money? Why money? What would it buy up here?

Without flinching he had heard how all the southern cities had been destroyed. Now he understood the meaning of those sudden gleams that lit the horizon during the night. And because this event had been the work of whites, Kakatso completely lost interest in it.

So his problem remained these four people he considered spoilers.

"Without you," said the woman, "we are going to perish."

And because Kakatso looked at her in surprise, she added, in a somewhat different tone: "We have no supplies at all and we are almost out of fuel."

"That's true," said the pilot.

"So," continued the woman, "if you don't help us find food, we will die."

Kakatso, with a sweeping gesture, indicated the forests and the lake: "There is wild game there and fish in the waters...."

"I don't have a gun or fishhooks," said the pilot. "And it's been a very long time since I came so far north."

He said this with a slightly abashed air and Kakatso saw clearly that the man's hands were too white; the skin had become too soft and smooth.

"I'll pay you whatever is necessary," said Mr. Perron.

"Can't you see, " said his wife, "that money doesn't interest him?"

Kakatso stood there, looking at them with his shining impassive eyes, his face unsmiling and his arms dangling at his sides.

"Say something," cried the woman. "Will you agree to help us?"

"We got away as best we could," said the pilot. "We gathered the attack on Montreal was coming and we were already at the airport when the warning sirens went off. But I couldn't take on enough fuel. There were other planes leaving too. I can't even take off again from this lake. Do you know if there is a supply cache near here?"

Throughout the northern forests pilots left emergency fuel caches for use when necessary. But if Kakatso knew of several such places he wasn't letting on in front of the intruders.

"I don't know," he said.

There was silence.

The whites looked at the Indian and desperately sought words to persuade him. But Kakatso did not move and said nothing. He had always fled the society of whites and dealt with them only when it was unavoidable. Why should he treat those who surfaced here now any differently? They were without food; the forest nourishes those who know how to take their share. This knowledge was such an instinctive part of an Indian's being that he couldn't realize how some people could lack it. He was sure that these people wanted to impose their needs on him and enslave him. All his Montagnais pride revolted against this thought. And yet, he could help them. Less than one hour away there was one of those meat caches of a thousand pounds of smoked moose, enough to see them through a winter. And the fish in the lake could be caught without much effort. Weaving a simple net of fine branches would do it, or a trap of bulrushes.

But he didn't move a muscle.

Only a single fixed thought possessed Kakatso, and it fascinated him. Down there, in the south, the whites had been destroyed. Never again would they reign over these forests. In killing each other, they had rid the land of their kind. Would the Indians be free again? All the Indians, even those on the reserves? Free to retake the forests?

And these four whites: could they be the last survivors?

Brothers, thought Kakatso, all my brothers: it is up to me to protect your new freedom.

"The cities," he finally said, "they have really been destroyed?"

"Yes," said the pilot.

"Nothing is left any more," said the woman. "Nothing at all. We saw the explosion from the plane. It was terrible. And the wind pushed us for a quarter of an hour. I thought we were going to crash."

"Nothing left," said the boy, "nobody left. Boom! One bomb did it."

He was delighted to feel himself the hero — a safe and sound hero — of such an adventure. He didn't seem able to imagine the destruction and death, only the spectacular explosion.

But the man called Perron had understood it well. He had been able to estimate the real power of the bomb.

"The whole city is destroyed," he said. "A little earlier, on the radio, we heard of the destruction of New York, then Toronto and Ottawa...."

"Many other cities too," added the pilot. "As far as I'm concerned, nothing is left of Canada, except perhaps the North Shore...."

"And it won't be for long," said Perron. "If we could get further up, further north. If we only had food and gasoline."

This time he took a roll of money out of his pocket and

unfolded five bills, a sum Kakatso had never handled at one time. Perron offered them to the Indian.

"Here. The only thing we ask you for is a little food and gas if you can get some. Then we could leave."

"When such a bomb explodes," said Kakatso without taking the bills, "does it kill all the whites?"

"Yes," said the pilot. "In any case, nearly all."

"One fell on Ottawa?"

"Yes."

"Everybody is dead there?"

"Yes. The city is small and the bomb was a big one. The reports indicate there were no survivors."

Kakatso nodded his head two or three times approvingly. Then he turned away and took his rifle which had been leaning on a rock. Slowly, aiming at the whites, he began to retreat into the forest.

"Where are you going?" cried the woman.

"Here," said the man. "Here's all my money. Come back!"

Only the pilot remained silent. With his sharp eyes he watched Kakatso.

When the Indian reached the edge of the forest it was the boy's turn. He began to sob pitifully, and the woman also began to cry.

"Don't leave," she cried. "Please, help us...."

For all of my people who cried, thought Kakatso, all who begged, who wanted to defend their rights for the past two hundred years: I take revenge for them all.

But he didn't utter another word.

And when the two men wanted to run after him to stop him, he put his rifle to his shoulder. The bullet nicked the pilot's ear. Then the men understood that it would be futile to insist, and Kakatso disappeared into the forest which enclosed him. Bent low, he skimmed the ground, using every bush for cover, losing himself in the undergrowth, melting into the forest where he belonged.

Later, having circled the lake, he rested on a promontory hidden behind many spreading cedars. He saw that the pilot was trying to take off to find food elsewhere.

But the tanks were nearly empty and when the plane

reached an altitude of a thousand feet the motor sputtered a bit, backfired and stopped.

The plane went into a nosedive.

When it hit the trees it caught fire.

In the morning Kakatso continued his trip towards the highlands.

He felt his first nausea the next day and vomited blood two days later. He vomited once at first, then twice, then a third time, and finally one last time.

The wind kept on blowing from the south, warm and mild.

The Wild
in Humanity
and Nature

Red Racer

Hugh Garner

The sun burned a hole in the sky and sent its thermal rays into the bare fields between the trees. The air was tense and still, as if every living organism was hoarding its strength for something vague but promised by the quiet day. Now and then Marcel Boudreau stopped his labors between the rows of yellowing leaves that topped the potato plants, and looked above the boundary of spruce and fir trees into the northwest sky.

Around the small cleared patch of farmland the wooded hills that skirt the Gaspé Coast had the appearance of a dirty patched fur rug laid in massive folds by some forgotten giant hand. From the ridges of the hills to the narrow valley in which the homestead lay, the thick forest growth was yellow, interspersed with the still heavy green of the coniferous trees.

The man leaned his weight upon the handle of his hoe and allowed his glance to drop from the sky to the rude clapboard house he had built against the wagon road. His wife and children moved about in the shade between the house and stable, the mumbled noises of their voices and laughter showing him their lack of apprehension. He was glad they did not share the concern he felt for the *something* that lay above the valley like the brooding anger of a god.

He went about his hoeing again with redoubled effort, letting the fatigue in his arms and the sweat under his shirt relieve him of the anxiety that he had felt since morning. When he reached the end of the row he paused and wiped his face with his handkerchief. He glanced towards the miniscule pasture in which his old horse was grazing and found corroboration for his feelings in the sight of the animal's stance: the horse stood in wary alertness, ears back, its forefeet pawing the turf in a corner near the fence.

Again he searched the washed blue of the sky, looking for signs of an approaching storm. There was nothing but a few thin wisps of cumulus against the brow of a hill, and the throbbing white disc of the sun. The August day followed almost two weeks of hot dry weather that had plagued Eastern Canada. Here, a few miles inland from the Gulf of St. Lawrence, the thick forests cut off all succoring breezes from the sea.

His throat felt parched and raw, and glad of the excuse his thirst gave him, he dropped the hoe and made his way towards the house. At his approach his wife looked up from her sewing and stared hard at his face. He knew by her glance that his apprehension was showing in his eyes.

"How's the potatoes looking, Marcel?" she asked in French, her tone still deferential even after twelve years of marriage.

"They're pretty dry. I pulled one a while ago though and they look all right."

"I wouldn't want them to spoil. We'd never get through the winter without potatoes."

"It seems to me we're in for a storm—there's a feeling of it in the air. We sure need some rain bad."

He finished the hoeing during the afternoon, and after

supper sat down beside the radio, listening to the nasal twang of a pseudo-cowboy from a New Brunswick station singing a lament while he chorded dismally on a mail-order guitar.

In the evenings when work was finished for the day it seemed to him that the past twelve years' effort had not been in vain. It had been heart-breaking at first, the effect of a long day's work dwarfed to insignificance by the seemingly im-mobile forest, but bit by bit — despite cold and hunger and privation—the small clearing had grown into the semblance of a farm.

Antoinette, his wife, was busy in a corner of the single first-floor room of the house bathing the youngest of their five children in a washtub on the floor. Apart from his wife and children his possessions were meager; a ten-year-old bay gelding of uncertain lineage, a scrub Holstein cow, a two-hundred-pound pig now fattening for the winter's meat, a few hens, a cat, and a half-wild collie bitch. He had fifty acres of paid-up land of which fifteen were cleared, a small weather-proof house, a log barn, three iron beds, a wood range, a radio and a sewing machine. Not a very impressive total of possessions in return for twelve years of labor, but enough to make a man feel a sense of achievement on an evening like this — a sense of fulfillment and security which thousands strove for in vain.

After the children had been put to bed upstairs Antoinette pulled a chair closer to the radio and began cutting patches from a pair of his old overalls with which to mend those belonging to his eldest boy.

They sat together in the gathering darkness, talking about the little things that filled their lives, grateful for the quiet of the room now that the children were asleep. The cowboy left the air and was replaced by the music of a Toronto dance orchestra carried by the network. The tympanic beat punctuated their conversation. When it grew too dark to see what she was doing, Antoinette lit a kerosene lamp and stood it on the sewing machine.

Another half-hour went by, then Marcel climbed the stairs

to bed, followed a few minutes later by his wife.

He awoke in the darkness with a foreboding that something was wrong. Stealing out of bed he picked up the clock from a chair and carried it into the grey light from the window. The hands pointed to three-twenty-five. He looked up into the sky and felt a sense of relief as he saw the stars making their silver pointed patterns in the ceiling of darkness.

Hurriedly pulling on his trousers and shoes he made his way down the stairs and out into the yard. The collie crept with stiff-legged indolence from beneath the steps and followed him as he walked across the narrow space to the barn. Everything was as it should be there. He circled the small building and stood for a moment staring into the pasture. The horse and cow were huddled together in uncommon intimacy in the corner nearest the road, their heads across the top rail of the fence. He thought, there may be bears around, and let his eyes sweep the surrounding ground looking for a tell-tale black shape. There was nothing to break the familiar profile of the fields.

He stood still, trying to pin-point the presentient feeling that filled the air, and then, suddenly, he knew what it was. He sniffed the night breeze and his heart stood still for the few seconds it took him to swing around. Down the length of the valley wafted the almost imperceptible odor of burning timber; the northland's smell of destruction, the red racer, a forest fire.

Looking up at the rim of the hills he now saw what he had been unable to see before: a faint pink line to the north-west, undulating incandescently against the deeper gloom of the night. He hurried into the house and awakened his wife, telling her in a few tense sentences what she should do. As she dressed hurriedly in the darkness he ran outside again to where the horse was standing in the pasture.

In half an hour they were ready to leave. The horse was tethered in the yard, harnessed to the wagon that contained the sewing machine, radio, the trussed-up pig and a pile of jumbled clothing upon which the children sat in sleep-broken expectancy. The cow lowed forlornly from the end of a rope by which she was tied to the wagon gate.

The upper air was now a mass of smoke, and vagrant wisps were carried down across the yard. From time to time a faint gossamer spread of powdered ash floated down upon the wagon. From the hills came a noise like a giant boiling cauldron, and a south-east breeze stirred the branches of the trees as it rushed into the vacuum left by the roaring flames of the racing fire.

Marcel worked out the position of the fire roughly, gauging its distance at not more than a mile. It appeared to be working its way swiftly across the range of hills in a direction that should carry its main sweep along the ridge that lay a mile north of his small homestead. From the sight now of the shooting flames with their plumed caps of black oily smoke he estimated its probable width as a mile and a half. If his calculations were correct it meant that the fire would skirt his farm to the north, leaving his property untouched. He said a silent prayer that this should happen, but he well knew the almost casual waywardness of a forest fire, that in one minute can shift its direction ninety degrees, and skipping a half-mile of forest, break out anew in another spot and with an entirely different destination. It was because of this knowledge of a fire's unpredictability that he had made the preparations to flee down the road through the hills to the coastal strip.

"I guess we'd better get going," he said to his wife, who was sitting on the wagon seat staring at the house as if reluctant to tear her eyes away.

"Not yet," she said slowly. "Maybe the fire won't come this way."

"We can't tell, and I don't want to take a chance."

"It took us so long to build it, Marcel. When I think of all the work we put into it, and the new kitchen stove we bought with the money you earned on the drive last spring..."

"We can replace a house and stove," he answered.

"Twelve years work..." she said, unable to finish the sentence; unable to say, "Twelve years work to be wiped out in a night."

He shrugged, pretending it was nothing. "We'll get the kids out anyway. We're young enough to start again."

She did not admit that she heard him. There was a faint overtone of hope in her voice as she said, "Even if the fire comes this way it may not cross the pasture."

He looked around him at the miles and miles of forest, among which his little farm was but the imprint of a heel in a field of grass. Then he said, "You're only wishing, 'Toinette. You know as well as me that it would jump the pasture as easy as the dog can jump the creek. It's no use hoping for a miracle—if the fire swings this way, the farm goes, and that's that."

The baby began to whimper in her blanket, and the mother shushed her, rocking back and forth on the narrow seat of the wagon. Marcel went to the horse's head to untie the rope that held the nervous animal to the clothes-line post, and as he did so he heard the truck coming along the road. He left the tethered horse and hurried round to the front of the house.

Headlights flickered through the trees and then became a bright glare as the truck rounded a bend fifty yards away. It was travelling fast, but before it came abreast of the house it slowed down and finally stopped. Marcel hurried over to the cab.

"Are you Boudreau?" an old man's voice asked in English.

"Yes."

"My name's McKendrick. I'm the fire warden from Ste. Gironde. We're picking up every man we can to fight that fire on the ridge. You'd better get in back with the others."

"What about my wife and kids? They're back behind the house in the wagon. I was just about to set off for the settlement."

"There's no need for them to leave here. That fire's been going dead east since yesterday morning. We're going to build a break up along the forks of the creek and try to back-flash the fire so that it'll burn itself out in the second-growth stuff over east of the third ridge. We need every man we can get, so you'd better get in the back."

"Just a minute while I tell my wife," Marcel said, running

back to the rear of the house.

He told his wife what the fire warden had said, feeling reassured now by the older man's words. He told her to keep the horse harnessed and ready to go, and to watch the fire. If it came into full view along the brow of the hill she was to set off for town as fast as she could go.

"I wish you could stay here with me," she said, although there was a note of resignation in her voice as she spoke.

"The warden says there's no danger here. We're only going up to the forks of the creek. I'll be back for breakfast," he said, hurrying away again through the faint illumination reflected by the north-west sky.

The back of the truck was already crowded with a silent mass of men, and they set off with a meshing of gears along the narrow road.

"Hello, Marcel," said a voice at his elbow.

He turned to see Omer Michaud, his nearest neighbor from five miles down the road, standing beside him.

"Hello, Omer. They got you, too, eh?"

The man nodded.

From Michaud he learned that the fire had begun the previous morning almost ten miles from its present position. It had been caused by a construction crew burning slash at the site of a new highway bridge. The small fire had crept through the grass and undergrowth beside the road, unnoticed by the construction men. Later on while they were gathered at their camp for lunch the small creeping flames had touched off a dried-out pile of cedar bark, and the fire had increased its size by immediate multiplication. When next it was seen it was advancing at a rapid pace through a stand of fir and hemlock, its feelers climbing thirty-foot trees like reversed lightning. From then on its size and speed had increased until it became the roaring killer now sweeping across the hills.

When the truck reached the end of the wide summer road the twenty-odd men aboard it jumped to the ground, and the fire warden handed out picks, shovels and axes for the job ahead of them. "There's two bulldozers on their way up from the settlement," he said, "but we'll have to make do with what we've got until they arrive."

He outlined his plan to them, tracing it on the ground with the point of a pick. In the reflected light from the dull-glowing sky the men stood around in a silent circle, their faces serious. Marcel recognized Pelletier the postmaster and three or four office workers from the mill. A pair of young men attired in light slacks and cotton jackets had the appearance of summer visitors. The others were farmers from around the settlement and a company woodsman or two.

The plan was a sound one. The fire was heading into a fork made by the junction of one creek with another. By widening the inner bank of one of the creeks several feet, it might be possible to induce the fire to take the path of least resistance across the other creek and down a long winding gully to where a burned-over valley could slow down and absorb the fire's hunger. This valley had suffered a fire several years before, and now its surface was covered with the sparse growth of small birch, poplar, wild cherry and stub maple that springs up on fire-ravaged land.

"Now, you know what to do, boys," McKendrick said. "Clear the trees and brush back at least ten feet from the south creek, and work the break as far along the stream as you can before she gets too hot to stay there. There's a crew of fifty men with pumps down in the valley and they'll check her after we send it their way. Young Bill Howlett in the tower on White Mountain is following the fire with his glasses, and he'll phone out for more help if it's needed. When you can't work any longer up there, make it towards the hills. We'll be over there with the truck.

The men followed each other up the narrow winter road a short distance until they reached the south creek. Without pausing they set to work with their axes on the trees and shrubs, letting them fall, and dragging them back from the creek bank. The dull red glow by which they worked was soon dimmed by the sun which sent a pale light through the ugly smoke that now stretched to the horizon.

Marcel threw himself into the job, knowing that all he

owned depended on their efforts to swing the fire to the east.
After an hour's gruelling work he looked behind him and
saw that they had succeeded only in advancing about
twenty-five yards from the forks. He thought, it isn't enough,
and he began hacking at the growth in a frenzy of desper-
ation.

The noise of the flames, and the sound of falling trees, now
almost deafened the small crew of men, and from the clouds
of acrid smoke fell burning embers the size of a man's hand,
which struck the ground with an explosive crack. The men
extinguished these with their boots or with the frantic slap-
pings of discarded shirts.

As the flames approached, the heat became unbearable,
and the men's faces were raw with it beneath their covering
of grime and sweat. Their efforts to widen a longer fire-break
along the creek bank had to be given up, and instead they
tried unsuccessfully to stifle the small pilot fires set up by the
burning brands. It was a losing fight. No sooner would one
fire be extinguished than its place would be taken by two or
more new ones breaking out behind them.

Soon they were forced to retreat before the searing heat
into the relative coolness of the scorched trees beyond the
creek. Most of the gang hurriedly made their way east
through the woods to the rendezvous with McKendrick on
the farther ridge. Michaud asked Marcel to go too, but
he shook his head, pointing down to the valley. Michaud
shrugged and hurried after the others.

Marcel watched the blinding line of the fire's advance as
it hurled itself through the trees. The dense smoke made
breathing difficult, but worse still was the lack of oxygen as
the gigantic combustion ate into the air supply surrounding
it. He lowered himself to the ground and began inching back
through the scrub, unmindful now of the shower of sparks
and embers that hurtled through the tops of the trees above
him, setting them alight with a crackling roar. As he crawled
along the ground he saw three foxes, a vixen and two pups,
racing across his path. With a new-found clarity he watched
the course of the foxes' flight. He was facing away from the

fire now, and the small red animals had passed, roughly, from west to east. Knowing that the intelligence of the fox would not allow her to lead her pups into the fire's path it could only mean one thing: their efforts to swing the fire to the east had been wasted, it had hurtled their shallow break almost without pause, and even now was eating down the valley towards his homestead.

For the first time he felt the hopelessness of his position— the lonely, trapped feeling of being deserted, and with no aid to look forward to. He crawled up a small knoll, hoping to put it between himself and the fire, before changing course in the direction of his home.

There was a frantic crashing of the undergrowth behind him, and he turned in time to see a lost member of the fire-fighting crew rushing along the advancing line of the fire. The man was one of the summer visitors, his once-grey slacks now black and ripped to ribbons around his bleeding legs, and his scorched and blackened face twisted with his efforts to breathe.

"Hey!" Marcel shouted, pushing himself up on his knees. "Come back! Come back!"

The man did not hear him. He made the vital mistake of trying to charge uphill before the flames instead of staying beneath them. Marcel watched with mounting horror as the man's crazed efforts to escape took him beneath a flaming arch of burning trees, which collapsed slowly, enveloping him in a fiery net. There was a piercing scream above the noise, then the flames roared on over the scene.

Sobbing with fatigue and fright Marcel crawled slowly over the height of the knoll, his handkerchief held to his face to protect it from the heat and smoke. He fell down the farther slope and lay against a tree while he batted out his smoldering overalls with blistered hands that were like the clumsy claws of a feebled bird.

When the flames began licking across the summit of the small rise he clambered to his feet and stumbled down the hill, bumping into the trees, freeing his feet from the tangle of long grass and undergrowth, unable now to see through the smoke and the matted curtains of his scorched and fused eyelashes.

His feet found the gravelled surface of a dried-up stream at the foot of the hill, and he made his way to the right along the creek bed. As his jarring steps carried him toward the valley floor the smoke thinned a little and the noise dimmed to a steady roar on the slopes above him. He knew that the fire would be slowed momentarily by its vertical path down the hill, so when his shoes splashed through the water of a spring he paused and laved his smarting eyes with the cool clear water. Then he flopped down in the wet earth and drank his fill, letting the gurgling water caress his blistered chest and back. Refreshed now, and feeling a new surge of strength, he hurried along the creek.

As he ran he watched a small fire springing up on the slope above him, caused by a vagrant spark or ember. The sight startled him, and he prayed that Antoinette and the children were already on their way down the road to the safety of the settlement. But then he noticed a peculiar thing about the blaze — it was crawling uphill in the direction of the main fire. He stared for a minute before he realized that the slope formed a natural flue from the valley, and the brisk wind that was rushing across the flatlands supplied the draft.

A crazy plan was formed in his mind at the sight. If he fired the whole length of the hill it might be possible to back-flash the main fire — that is, lay waste the slope by burning its covering of trees and vegetation so that the advancing flames would stop short on the summit for lack of combustible material in their path. In this way the fire could be made to continue east towards the spot chosen by the fire-warden and his crews, and where they were preparing and widening a long fire-break.

It was worth the attempt only if he could be sure that his wife and family were safely out of the way. There was the great danger that his efforts might be in vain, and the time wasted make it impossible to flee when the fire began its race across the valley. And there was the probability that the back-flash might become the forerunner of the main fire and thus advance its line the few hundred yards it needed to bridge the distance between its position on the hill and the valley floor.

He stood a moment in fearful hesitation before making up his mind, gambling his safety and the safety of his family against the possible saving of his house and land. Then, his life and future depending on the cast of a die, he ran several yards down the bank of the trickling stream and gathered an armful of spruce bark from a brown flattened pile he had left there when peeling pulpwood in the spring.

Twisting some in his hand he ran up the few feet of slope and held it in the flames until it smoldered and took fire. He inched his way through the trees, touching his rough torch to the dry crackling underbrush.

It caught fire slowly at first, but as he moved along he turned his head and watched the thin crawling pattern of flames take hold and begin to roar through the trees. He felt an exultation as he twisted new torches from the bundle of bark under his arm, lighting them from the fires he had already kindled.

As he advanced along the base of the slope he could hear the crackling destruction behind him as the fire accelerated up the hill. It had a new music in his ears, of aid and succor, as its sound supplied the counterpoint to the enveloping roar of the advancing fire from above.

In a few minutes the hill became an inferno, the flames rushing through the trees with a terrible unleashing of thermal power, reducing the thirty-year growth of fir and spruce to blackened poles and smoking ash in a matter of minutes. The man stood back behind the small creek amazed at the destruction he had caused.

At times a slackening of the breeze would cause the flames to flicker almost gently beneath the wide ceiling of smoke, and he would watch with heart-stopping expectancy for the fire to change course and rush down upon him.

As the fire climbed the hill he moved along the creek bank extinguishing small blazes that had sprung up behind it, stamping them into the ground as he executed a joyful dance upon the earth. For a long time it was touch and go. The two blazes advanced against each other, each striving for mastery. Behind the one he had made was a narrow fifty-yard strip of ravished earth that might prove ineffective in stopping the fire's main advance. He watched the clash, his tongue between his teeth and his blistered hands clenching at his sides. The two fires met with a giant roar, and the flames leaped high against the pall of smoke. Then, slowly, the red leaping fires on the slope sunk to the charred and blackened ground, and the blaze swung away to the east and ate its way across the hills.

After another half-hour had passed, and he had stamped out all the small borderline blazes, he left the scene of his triumph and pushed his way headlong through the valley trees towards his farm.

Antoinette met him at the gate, her face wearing a tired smile behind her smoke-smeared features. She was inarticulate with happiness as she took his arm and led him into the house. He sat on a chair and allowed her to film his face and hands with Vaseline, staring through the window at the fire as it retreated east along the top of the hills. She made a pot of tea, almost caressing the shiny stove as she went about her task, her face flushed from the heat and happiness that rose about her. When they had finished their tea Marcel went into the yard, untied the horse and cow, and liberated the trussed-up pig, driving them into the small stable. The children were once more playing around the house as Antoinette carried the bundles of clothing from the wagon.

He asked her, "Why did you stay here when you saw the fire on the slope?" trying to make his voice gruff and authoritative.

She did not answer him, but instead went quickly about her work, stopping now and then to stare at the burning hills. Once, when Marcel looked into her face he saw that there were two tear streaks down the sides of her nose, so he made himself busy carrying the radio and sewing machine into the house.

Later on he pulled on a fresh shirt and made ready to leave again for the fire-break the crews were building above the hills across the valley. His wife tried to prevent him going, but there was a light in his eyes that she had never seen before.

He said his good-byes, warning the oldest children not to go near the still-smoldering patch above the farm, and set off towards the road. The fire was now an impersonal thing that had slowed to a crawl through the bush and scrub along the hills, its terror gone with its defeat. As he passed the potato patch, from habit he pulled one of the plants, and looked into the north-west sky for a sign of rain. Behind the greying smoke several horse tails of cirrus cloud were sweeping across the sky, heralding the approach of a storm. He laughed to himself as he remembered his apprehension of the day before, and he hurried up the road towards the waiting fire-crews, afraid that the rain might cheat him of his victory.

The Blackwater Pot

Charles G. D. Roberts

The lesson of fear was one which Henderson learned late. He learned it well, however, when the time came. And it was Blackwater Pot that taught him.

Sluggishly, reluctantly, impotently, the spruce logs followed one another round and round the circuit of the great stone pot. The circling water within the pot was smooth and deep and black, but streaked with foam. At one side a gash in the rocky rim opened upon the sluicing current of the river, which rushed on, quivering and seething, to plunge with a roar into the terrific cauldron of the falls. Out of that thunderous cauldron, filled with huge tramplings and the shriek of tortured torrents, rose a white curtain of spray, which every now and then swayed upward and drenched the green birches which grew about the rim of the pot. For the break in the rim, which caught at the passing current and sucked it into the slow swirls of Blackwater Pot, was not a dozen feet from the lip of the falls.

Henderson sat at the foot of a ragged white birch which leaned from the upper rim of the pot. He held his pipe unlighted, while he watched the logs with a half-fascinated stare. Outside, in the river, he saw them in a clumsy panic haste, wallowing down the white rapids to their awful plunge. When a log came close along shore its fate hung for a second or two in doubt. It might shoot straight on, over the lip, into the wavering curtain of spray and vanish into the horror of the cauldron. Or, at the last moment, the eddy might reach out stealthily and drag it into the sullen wheeling procession within the pot. All that it gained here, however, was a terrible kind of respite, a breathing-space of agonized suspense. As it circled around, and came again to the opening by which it had entered, it might continue on another eventless revolution, or it might, according to the whim of the eddy, be cast forth once more, irretrievably, into the clutch of the awful sluice. Sometimes two logs, after a pause in what seemed like a secret death-struggle, would crowd each other out and go over the falls together. And sometimes, on the other hand, all would make the circuit safely again and again. But always, at the cleft in the rim of the pot, there was the moment of suspense, the shuddering, terrible panic.

It was this recurring moment that seemed to fasten itself balefully upon Henderson's imagination, so that he forgot to smoke. He had looked into the Blackwater before, but never when there were any logs in the pot. Moreover, on this particular morning, he was overwrought with weariness. For a little short of three days he had been at the utmost tension of body, brain, and nerve, in hot but wary pursuit of a desperado whom it was his duty, as deputy-sheriff of his county, to capture and bring to justice.

This outlaw, a French half-breed, known through the length and breadth of the wild backwoods county as "Red Pichot", was the last but one — and accounted the most dangerous—of a band which Henderson had undertaken to break up. Henderson had been deputy for two years, and owed his appointment primarily to his pre-eminent fitness for this very task. Unacquainted with fear, he was at the same time unrivalled through the backwoods counties for his subtle woodcraft, his sleepless endurance, and his cunning.

It was two years now since he had set his hand to the business. One of the gang had been hanged. Two were in the penitentiary, on life sentence. Henderson had justified his appointment to every one except himself. But while Pichot and his gross-witted tool, "Bug" Mitchell, went unhanged, he felt himself on probation, if not shamed. Mitchell he despised. But Pichot, the brains of the gang, he honoured with a personal hatred that held a streak of rivalry. For Pichot, though a beast for cruelty and treachery, and with the murder of a woman on his black record — which placed him, according to Henderson's ideas, in a different category from a mere killer of men — was at the same time a born leader and of a courage none could question. Some chance dash of Scotch Highland blood in his mixed veins had set a mop of hot red hair above his black, implacable eyes and cruel, dark face. It had touched his villainies, too, with an imagination which made them the more atrocious. And Henderson's hate for him as a man was mixed with respect for the adversary worthy of his powers.

Reaching the falls, Henderson had been forced to acknowledge that, once again, Pichot had outwitted him on the trail. Satisfied that his quarry was by this time far out of reach among the tangled ravines on the other side of Two Mountains, he dismissed the two tired river-men who constituted his posse, bidding them go on down the river to Greensville and wait for him. It was his plan to hunt alone for a couple of days in the hope of catching his adversary off guard. He had an ally, unsuspected and invaluable, in a long-legged, half-wild youngster of a girl, who lived alone with her father in a clearing about a mile below the falls, and regarded Henderson with a childlike hero-worship. This shy little savage, whom all the Settlement knew as "Baisley's Sis", had an intuitive knowledge of the wilderness and the trails which rivalled even Henderson's accomplished woodcraft; and the indomitable deputy "set great store", as he would have put it, by her friendship. He would go down presently to the clearing and ask some questions of the child. But first he wanted to do a bit of thinking. To think the better, the better to collect his tired and scattered wits, he had stood his Winchester carefully upright between two spruce saplings, filled his pipe, lighted it with relish, and seated himself under the old birch where he could look straight down upon the wheeling logs in Blackwater Pot.

It was while he was looking down into the terrible eddy that his efforts to think failed him and his pipe went out, and his interest in the fortunes of the captive logs gradually took the hold of a nightmare upon his overwrought imagination. One after one he would mark, snatched in by the capricious eddy and held back a little while from its doom. One after one he would see crowded out again, by inexplicable whim, and hurled on into the raging horror of the falls. He fell to personifying this captive log or that, endowing it with sentience, and imagining its emotions each time it circled shuddering past the cleft in the rim, once more precariously reprieved.

At last, either because he was more deeply exhausted than he knew, or because he had fairly dropped asleep with his eyes open and his fantastic imaginings had slipped into a veritable dream, he felt himself suddenly become identified with one of the logs. It was one which was just drawing around to the fateful cleft. Would it win past once more? No; it was too far out! It felt the grasp of the outward suction, soft and insidious at first, then resistless as the falling of a mountain. With straining nerves and pounding heart Henderson strove to hold it back by sheer will and the wrestling of his eyes. But it was no use. Slowly the head of the log turned outward from its circling fellows, quivered for a moment in the cleft, then shot smoothly forth into the sluice. With a groan Henderson came to his senses, starting up and catching instinctively at the butt of the heavy Colt in his belt. At the same instant the coil of a rope settled over his shoulders, pinioning his arms to his sides, and he was jerked backwards with a violence that fairly lifted him over the projecting root of the birch. As he fell his head struck a stump; and he knew nothing more.

When Henderson came to his senses he found himself in a most bewildering position. He was lying face downwards along a log, his mouth pressed upon the rough bark. His arms and legs were in the water, on either side of the log. Other logs moved past him sluggishly. For a moment he thought himself still in the grip of his nightmare, and he struggled to wake himself. The struggle revealed to him that he was bound fast upon the log. At this his wits cleared up, with a pang that was more near despair than anything he had ever known. Then his nerve steadied itself back into its wonted control.

He realized what had befallen him. His enemies had back-trailed him and caught him off his guard. He was just where, in his awful dream, he had imagined himself as being. He was bound to one of the logs down in the great stone pot of Blackwater Eddy.

For a second or two the blood in his veins ran ice, as he braced himself to feel the log lurch out into the sluice and plunge into the trampling of the abyss. Then he observed that the other logs were overtaking and passing him. His log, indeed, was not moving at all. Evidently, then, it was being held by some one. He tried to look around, but found himself so fettered that he could only lift his face a few inches from the log. This enabled him to see the whole surface of the eddy and the fateful cleft, and out across the raving torrents into the white curtain that swayed above the cauldron. But he could not, with the utmost twisting and stretching of his neck, see more than a couple of feet up the smooth stone sides of the pot.

As he strained on his bonds he heard a harsh chuckle behind him; and the log, suddenly loosed with a jerk which showed him it had been held by a pike-pole, began to move. A moment later the sharp, steel-armed end of the pike-pole came down smartly on the forward end of the log, within a dozen inches of Henderson's head, biting a secure hold. The log again came to a stop. Slowly, under pressure from the other end of the pike-pole, it rolled outward, submerging Henderson's right shoulder, and turning his face till he could see all the way up the sides of the pot.

What he saw, on a ledge about three feet above the water, was Red Pichot, holding the pike-pole and smiling down upon him smoothly. On the rim above squatted Bug Mitchell, scowling, and gripping his knife as if he thirsted to settle up all scores on the instant. Imagination was lacking in Mitchell's make-up; and he was impatient — so far as he dared to be — of Pichot's fantastic procrastinatings.

When Henderson's eyes met the evil, smiling glance of his enemy they were steady and cold as steel. To Henderson, who had always, in every situation, felt himself master, there remained now no mastery but that of his own will, his own spirit. In his estimation there could be no death so dreadful but that to let his spirit cower before his adversary would be tenfold worse. Helpless though he was, in a position that was ignominiously and grotesquely horrible, and with the imminence of an appalling doom close before his eyes, his nerve never failed him. With cool contempt and defiance he met Red Pichot's smile.

"I've always had an idee," said the half-breed, presently, in a smooth voice that penetrated the mighty vibrations of the falls, "ez how a chap on a log could paddle roun' this yere eddy fer a deuce of a while afore he'd hev to git sucked out into the sluice!"

As a theory this was undoubtedly interesting. But Henderson made no answer.

"I've held that idee," continued Pichot, after a civil pause, "though I hain't never yet found a man, nor a woman nuther, as was willin' to give it a fair trial. But I feel sure ye're the man to oblige me. I've left yer arms kinder free, leastways from the elbows down, an' yer legs also, more or less, so's ye'll be able to paddle easy-like. The walls of the pot's all worn so smooth, below high-water mark, there's nothin' to ketch on to, so there'll be nothin' to take off yer attention. I'm hopin' ye'll give the matter a right fair trial. But ef ye gits tired an' feels like givin' up, why, don't consider my feelin's. There's the

falls awaitin'. An' I ain't agoin' to bear no grudge ef ye don't
quite come up to my expectations of ye.''

As Pichot ceased his measured harangue he jerked his
pike-pole loose. Instantly the log began to forge forward,
joining the reluctant procession. For a few moments Henderson felt like shutting his eyes and his teeth and letting
himself go on with all speed to the inevitable doom. Then,
with scorn of the weak impulse, he changed his mind. To the
last gasp he would maintain his hold on life, and give fortune
a chance to save him. When he could no longer resist, then it
would be Fate's responsibility, not his. The better to fight the
awful fight that was before him, he put clear out of his mind
the picture of Red Pichot and Mitchell perched on the brink
above, smoking, and grinning down upon the writhings of
their victim. In a moment, as his log drew near the cleft, he
had forgotten them. There was room now in all his faculties
for but one impulse, one consideration.

The log to which he was bound was on the extreme outer
edge of the procession, and Henderson realized that there
was every probability of its being at once crowded out the
moment it came to the exit. With a desperate effort he
succeeded in catching the log nearest to him, pushing it
ahead, and at last, just as they came opposite the cleft,
steering his own log into its place. The next second it shot
quivering forth into the sluice, and Henderson, with a sudden cold sweat jumping out all over him, circled slowly past
the awful cleft. A shout of ironical congratulation came to
him from the watchers on the brink above. But he hardly
heard it, and heeded it not at all. He was striving frantically,
paddling forward with one hand and backward with the
other, to steer his sluggish, deep-floating log from the outer
to the inner circle. He had already observed that to be on the
outer edge would mean instant doom for him, because the
outward suction was stronger underneath than on the surface, and his weighted log caught its force before the others
did. His arms were so bound that only from the elbows down
could he move them freely. He did, however, by a struggle
which left him gasping, succeed in working in behind

another log—just in time to see that log, too, sucked out into the abyss, and himself once more on the deadly outer flank of the circling procession.

This time Henderson did not know whether the watchers on the brink laughed or not as he won past the cleft. He was scheming desperately to devise some less exhausting tactics. Steadily and rhythmically, but with his utmost force, he back-paddled with both hands and feet, till the progress of his log was almost stopped. Then he succeeded in catching yet another log as it passed and manoeuvring in behind it. By this time he was halfway around the pot again. Yet again, by his desperate back-paddling, he checked his progress, and presently, by most cunning manipulation, managed to edge in behind yet another log, so that when he again came round to the cleft there were two logs between him and doom. The outermost of these, however, was dragged instantly forth into the fury of the sluice, thrust forward, as it was, by the grip of the suction upon Henderson's own deep log. Feeling himself on the point of utter exhaustion, he nevertheless continued back-paddling, and steering and working inward, till he had succeeded in getting three files of logs between himself and the outer edge. Then, almost blind and with the blood roaring so loud in his ears that he could hardly hear the trampling of the falls, he hung on his log, praying that strength might flow back speedily into his veins and nerves.

Not till he had twice more made the circuit of the pot, and twice more seen a log sucked out from his very elbow to leap into the white horror of the abyss, did Henderson stir. The brief stillness, controlled by his will, had rested him for the moment. He was cool now, keen to plan, cunning to husband his forces. Up to the very last second that he could he would maintain his hold on life, counting always on the chance of the unexpected.

With now just one log remaining between himself and death, he let himself go past the cleft, and saw that one log go out. Then, being close to the wall of the pot, he tried to delay his progress by clutching at the stone with his left hand and by dragging upon it with his foot. But the stone surface was worn so smooth by the age-long polishing of the eddy that these efforts availed him little. Before he realized it he was almost round again, and only by the most desperate struggle did he succeed in saving himself. There was no other log near by this time for him to seize and thrust forward in his place. It was simply a question of his restricted paddling, with hands and feet, against the outward draught of the current. For nearly a minute the log hung in doubt just before the opening, the current sucking at its head to turn it outward, and Henderson paddling against it not only with hands and feet, but with every ounce of will and nerve that his body contained. At last, inch by inch, he conquered. His log moved past the gate of death; and dimly, again, that ironical voice came down to him, piercing the roar.

Once past, Henderson fell to back-paddling again—not so violently now—till other logs came by within his reach and he could work himself into temporary safety behind them. He was soon forced to the conviction that if he strove at just a shade under his utmost he was able to hold his own and keep one log always between himself and the opening. But what was now his utmost, he realized, would very soon be far beyond his powers. Well, there was nothing to do but to keep on trying. Around and around, and again and again around the terrible, smooth, deliberate circuit he went, sparing himself every ounce of effort that he could, and always shutting his eyes as the log beside him plunged out into the sluice. Gradually, then, he felt himself becoming stupefied by the ceaselessly recurring horror, with the prolonged suspense between. He must sting himself back to the full possession of his faculties by another burst of fierce effort. Fiercely he caught at log after log, without a let-up, till, luck having favoured him for once, he found himself on the inner instead of the outer edge of the procession. Then an idea flashed into his fast-clouding brain, and he cursed himself for not having thought of it before. At the very centre of the eddy, of course, there must be a sort of core of stillness. By a vehement struggle he attained it and avoided crossing it. Working gently and warily he kept the log right across the axis of the eddy, where huddled a crowd of chips and sticks. Here the log turned slowly, very slowly, on its own centre; and for a few seconds of exquisite relief Henderson let himself sink into a sort of lethargy. He was roused by a sudden shot, and the spat of a heavy bullet into the log about three inches before his head. Even through the shaking thunder of the cataract he thought he recognized the voice of his own heavy Colt; and the idea of that tried weapon being turned against himself filled him with childish rage. Without lifting his head he lay and cursed, grinding his teeth impotently. A few seconds later came another shot, and this time the ball went into the log just before his right arm. Then he understood, and woke up. Pichot was a dead shot. This was his intimation that Henderson must get out into the procession again. At the centre of the eddy he was not sufficiently entertaining to his executioners. The idea of being shot in the head had not greatly disturbed him — he had felt as if it would be rather restful, on the whole. But the thought of getting a bullet in his arm, which would merely disable him and deliver him over helpless to the outdraught, shook him with something near a panic. He fell to paddling with all his remaining strength, and drove his log once more into the horrible circuit. The commendatory remarks with which Pichot greeted this move went past his ears unheard.

Up to this time there had been a strong sun shining down into the pot, and the trees about its rim had stood unstirred by any wind. Now, however, a sudden darkness settled over everything, and sharp, fitful gusts drew in through the cleft, helping to push the logs back. Henderson was by this time so near fainting from exhaustion that his wits were losing their clearness. Only his horror of the fatal exit, the raving sluice, the swaying white spray-curtain, retained its keenness. As to all else he was growing so confused that he hardly realized the way those great indrawing gusts, laden with spray, were helping him. He was paddling and steering and manoeu-vring for the inner circuit almost mechanically now. When suddenly the blackness about him was lit with a blue glare, and the thunder crashed over the echoing pot with an explosion that outroared the falls, he hardly noted it. When the skies seemed to open, letting down the rain in torrents, with a wind that almost blew it level, it made no difference to him. He went on paddling dully, indifferent to the bumping of the logs against his shoulders.

But to this fierce storm, which almost bent double the trees around the rim of the pot, Red Pichot and Mitchell were by no means so indifferent. About sixty or seventy yards below the falls they had a snug retreat which was also an outlook. It was a cabin built in a recess of the wall of the gorge, and to be reached only by a narrow pathway easy of defence. When the storm broke in its fury Pichot sprang to his feet.

"Let's git back to the Hole," he cried to his companion, knocking the fire out of his pipe. "We kin watch just as well from there, an' see the beauty slide over when his time comes."

Pichot led the way off through the straining and hissing trees, and Mitchell followed, growling but obedient. And Henderson, faint upon his log in the raving tumult, knew nothing of their going.

They had not been gone more than two minutes when a drenched little dark face, with black hair plastered over it in wisps, peered out from among the lashing birches and gazed down anxiously into the pot. At the sight of Henderson on his log, lying quite close to the edge, and far back from the dreadful cleft, the terror in the wild eyes gave way to inexpressible relief. The face drew back; and an instant later a bare-legged child appeared, carrying the pike-pole which Pichot had tossed into the bushes. Heedless of the sheeting volleys of the rain and the fierce gusts which whipped her dripping homespun petticoat about her knees, she clambered skilfully down the rock wall to the ledge whereon Pichot had stood. Bracing herself carefully, she reached out with the pike-pole, which, child though she was, she evidently knew how to use.

Henderson was just beginning to recover from his daze, and to notice the madness of the storm, when he felt something strike sharply on the log behind him. He knew it was the impact of a pike pole, and he wondered, with a kind of scornful disgust, what Pichot could be wanting of him now. He felt the log being dragged backwards, then held close against the smooth wall of the pot. A moment more and his bonds were being cut — but laboriously, as if with a small knife and by weak hands. Then he caught sight of the hands, which were little and brown and rough, and realized, with a great burst of wonder and tenderness, that old Baisley's "Sis", by some miracle of miracles, had come to his rescue. In a few seconds the ropes fell apart, and he lifted himself, to see the child stooping down with anxious adoration in her eyes.

"Sis!" he cried. "You!"

"Oh, Mr. Henderson, come quick!" she panted. "They may git back any minit." And clutching him by the shoulder, she tried to pull him up by main strength. But Henderson needed no urging. Life, with the return of hope, had surged back into nerve and muscle; and in hardly more time than it takes to tell it, the two had clambered side by side to the rim of the pot and darted into the covert of the tossing trees.

No sooner were they in hiding than Henderson remembered his rifle and slipped back to get it. His enemies had not discovered it. It had fallen into the moss, but the well-oiled, perfect-fitting chamber had kept its cartridges dry. With that weapon in his hands Henderson felt himself once more master of the situation. Weariness and apprehension together slipped from him, and one purpose took complete possession of him. He would settle with Red Pichot right there, on the spot where he had been taught the terrible lesson of fear. He felt that he could not really feel himself a man again unless he could settle the whole score before the sun of that day should set.

The rain and wind were diminishing now; the lightning was a mere shuddering gleam over the hill-tops beyond the river; and the thunder no longer made itself heard above the trampling of the falls. Henderson's plans were soon laid. Then he turned to Sis, who stood silent and motionless close at his side, her big, alert, shy eyes watching like a hunted deer's the trail by which Red Pichot might return. She was trembling in her heart at every moment that Henderson lingered within that zone of peril. But she would not presume to suggest any move.

Suddenly Henderson turned to her and laid an arm about her little shoulders.

"You saved my life, kid!" he said, softly. "How ever did you know I was down there in that hell?"

"I jest *knowed* it was you, when I seen Red Pichot an' Bug Mitchell a-trackin' some one," answered the child, still keeping her eyes on the trail, as if it was her part to see that Henderson was not again taken unawares. "I *knowed* it was you, Mister Henderson, an' I followed 'em; an' oh, I seen it all, I seen it all, an' I most died because I hadn't no gun. But I'd 'ave killed 'em both, some day, sure, ef — ef they hadn't went away! But they'll be back now right quick."

Henderson bent and kissed her wet black head, saying, "Bless you, kid! You an' me'll always be pals, I reckon!"

At the kiss the child's face flushed, and, for one second forgetting to watch the trail, she lifted glowing eyes to his. But he was already looking away.

"Come on," he muttered. "This ain't no place for you an' me *yet*."

Making a careful circuit through the thick undergrowth, swiftly but silently as two wild-cats, the strange pair gained a covert close beside the trail by which Pichot and Mitchell would return to the rim of the pot. Safely ambuscaded, Henderson laid a hand firmly on the child's arm, resting it there for two or three seconds, as a sign of silence.

Minute after minute went by in the intense stillness. At last the child, whose ears were even keener than Henderson's, caught her breath with a little indrawing gasp and looked up at her companion's face. Henderson understood; and every muscle stiffened. A moment later and he, too, heard the oncoming tread of hurried footsteps. Then Pichot went by at a swinging stride, with Mitchell skulking obediently at his heels.

Henderson half raised his rifle, and his face turned grey

and cold like steel. But it was no part of his plan to shoot even Red Pichot in the back. From the manner of the two ruffians it was plain that they had no suspicion of the turn which affairs had taken. To them it was as sure as two and two make four that Henderson was still on his log in the pot, if he had not already gone over into the cauldron. As they reached the rim Henderson stepped out into the trail behind them, his gun balanced ready like a trapshooter's.

As Pichot, on the very brink, looked down into the pot and saw that his victim was no longer there, he turned to Mitchell with a smile of mingled triumph and disappointment.

But, on the instant, the smile froze on his face. It was as if he had felt the cold, grey gaze of Henderson on the back of his neck. Some warning, certainly, was flashed to that mysterious sixth sense which the people of the wild, man or beast, seem sometimes to be endowed with. He wheeled like lightning, his revolver seeming to leap up from his belt with the same motion. But in the same fraction of a second that his eyes met Henderson's they met the white flame-spurt of Henderson's rifle — and then, the dark.

As Pichot's body collapsed, it toppled over the rim into Blackwater Pot and fell across two moving logs. Mitchell had thrown up his hands straight above his head when Pichot fell, knowing instantly that that was his only hope of escaping the same fate as his leader's.

One look at Henderson's face, however, satisfied him that he was not going to be dealt with on the spot, and he set his thick jaw stolidly. Then his eyes wandered down into the pot, following the leader whom, in his way, he had loved if ever he had loved any one or anything. Fascinated, his stare followed the two logs as they journeyed around, with Pichot's limp form, face upwards, sprawled across them. They reached the cleft, turned, and shot forth into the raving of the sluice, and a groan of horror burst from "Bug's" lips. By this Henderson knew what had happened, and, to his immeasurable self-scorn, a qualm of remembered fear caught sickeningly at his heart. But nothing of this betrayed itself in his face or voice.

"Come on, Mitchell!" he said, briskly. "I'm in a hurry. You

jest step along in front, an' see ye keep both hands well up over yer head, or ye'll be savin' the county the cost o' yer rope. Step out, now.''

He stood aside, with Sis at his elbow, to make room. As Mitchell passed, his hands held high, a mad light flamed up into his sullen eyes, and he was on the point of springing, like a wolf, at his captor's throat. But Henderson's look was cool and steady, and his gun held low. The impulse flickered out in the brute's dull veins. But as he glanced at Sis he suddenly understood that it was she who had brought all this to pass. His black face snarled upon her like a wolf's at bay, with an inarticulate curse more horrible than any words could make it. With a shiver the child slipped behind Henderson's back and hid her face.

"Don't be skeered o' him, kid, not one little mite," said Henderson, gently. "He ain't agoin' to trouble this earth no more. An' I'm goin' to get yer father a job, helpin' me, down somewheres near Greensville — because I couldn't sleep nights knowin' ye was runnin' round anywheres near that hell-hole yonder!''

The
Weasel Skin

Will R. Bird

The shack was a blur in a waste of snow and scattered scrub tangles, a desolate blot of darkness in the discoloured wilderness. It had been erected when a group of men were there cutting pulpwood, which they sledded to the coast, two miles distant. It was a northern part of Newfoundland and away from the settlements.

Inside the shack three men were sleeping, rolled snugly in blankets. They were amateur trappers and had thought they would make a small fortune by enduring the winter cold and setting snares and traps. But the weather had been against them. Blinding snowstorms had caught them unawares and had blotted out all signs of the trail they had used. There were more than twenty traps they could not find.

A light wind whispered through the scrub, a chill wind filled with a sense tf thaw. Spring was on the way for it was the month of March. The wind pulled lightly at the shack door, which made no sound on its leather hinges, and its breath fanned an ember that had fallen from the sheet-iron stove when one of the sleepers had drowsily replenished the fire. The ember reddened and a tiny spiral of smoke rose toward the pole roof. Like an evil winking eye, the glow increased or darkened under pressure of the draught along the floor. Finally it burst into small flames.

After a time one of the sleepers stirred and strangled with smoke. He struggled from his blankets, gasping and choking.

"Fire!"

His yell was filled with fear. He plunged, hands over his eyes, to the door and wrenched it open. On the instant the interior was a roaring furnace.

An hour later the three men turned from a heap of smoking debris and began to journey southward. They had saved a rifle, an axe, a cooking pot and frypan, a few provisions. That was all. Their entire winter's catch of fur had vanished in foul smoke.

"If you hadn't kicked the door open we could have got her out," Hawker said bitterly. He was a lean, dark man with straight black hair and a hatchet face. He had roamed up and down the east coast, working at various jobs, and had the reputation of being both a liar and a loafer.

"There was too much fire also," Dubuc joined in. "You fixed it twice for sure. The last time you full her too full." He was a short, swarthy man, a hardened veteran of the bush and traplines.

The third man made no answer to their accusations. He was stolid-faced and heavy-limbed, giving an impression of oxlike strength and intelligence. His name was Jim Crowdy and he came from Angel Cove. Hawker had induced him to come after hearing about his ability in the bush, and his almost childlike credulity. A boat from the Cove had taken them north and landed them in a small inlet from which they had travelled by compass.

"We've just got two blankets," Hawker said, gazing at their salvage.

"I fetched mine out," said Jim quietly.

"You did?" snarled Hawker. "Where'd you put it? Them two is mine. And I also brought out the rifle and a sack of biscuits."

"I got the axe," Dubuc said, "the frypan, an' some bacon."

Jim gazed at them. "I just got the kettle and tea," he said. "I couldn't find the tea right off because it had been knocked on the floor, but I knew we'd need it as much as anything."

"An' that's all we got, is it?" Hawker spat into the snow and looked at Dubuc.

"That's all," Dubuc answered.

Crowdy said nothing. His mind was still a chaos. The fire had startled him mightily. In the swirling smoke he had seen Hawker thrust a tin of beans inside his jacket and now there was no tin in the heap on the snow.

Each man picked up his own load and they started off across the snow, with Hawker leading. It was back-breaking labor for the snows were rotten with subtle thaws and heavy with moisture. Not one of them had thought to snatch away the long, light sled leaned against the end of the shack. They were soon sweating, for they had only been making the rounds of twenty-two traps and snares, and Hawker had invented many excuses not to take his regular turns. They plodded at a snail's pace, irritably conscious of their perspiration.

Yet it was imperative they make as much time as possible. There was a drab sky and the air was filled with hints of a storm. There was no hope of their finding a shelter. The open spaces stretched endlessly, their dirty whiteness a ghastly waste, their heavy stillness weird and chilling.

"If it's all like this," Hawker gritted over his shoulder, "we'll need a week to reach the coast."

"It's four days from the lake," Dubuc responded. "We've got to push on much faster."

"But we should stop noons to make tea," Crowdy said. "It doesn't take long to boil a kettle. I've got enough matches and tea's a grand help."

A single snowflake drifted down before Hawker, and he quickened his pace.

"In an hour," he said tersely, "it'll be so thick you can't see."

"There's bush," Dubuc pointed ahead. "There's a hollow."

The spot he indicated was nearly a mile away, a mass of greenery showing solid in the dirty-white wilderness. They travelled with all possible speed, yet before half the distance had been covered the storm was on them. Snow filled the air, blinding them. It swirled and eddied about them. It had suddenly turned colder and a wind was rising.

Hawker kept in the lead, toiling doggedly. Each man was a white-sheeted figure, aching with fatigue, and Dubuc called out sharply that they were not holding to the right direction.

"You find it then," Hawker yelled, and the shorter man plunged past him without a word.

Crowdy, labouring behind Dubuc, bumped into Hawker, who snarled an oath and then elbowed past Crowdy to get next to Dubuc. The storm tore at their cheeks and half-blinded them, but they finally slithered into the hollow — a small ravine piled deep with snow.

Stunted spruce grew thickly. They wallowed into the largest thicket and cleared a refuge, interlacing brush to form a roof. Dead undergrowth furnished an abundance of fuel and they built a fire. Smoke encircled them in choking gusts but they kept adding wood. They chilled as soon as the fire died down and they ceased exertions.

The day seemed endless. They were cramped in a small space, and the heat of their fire heated snow in the bush tops above them so that the brush dripped continuously. Crowdy made tea at noon and they had fried bacon. Dubuc sliced scanty portions.

"She's got to last," he said.

He and Hawker, warmed by the tea and bacon, began to talk about their loss of fur and to quarrel over its worth.

"I'd have had five hundred clear," Hawker said with an oath. "An' I needed that money bad."

"The same wit' me," Dubuc said angrily. "Me, I mak' one note for t'ree hun'erd wit' a man."

They did not speak to Crowdy.

It was night before the storm lessened, and then a stronger wind piled the new snow in immense drifts.

At dawn they climbed from the ravine and resumed their

struggle east and southward. The going was far more difficult than on the previous day and it was intensely cold. The sky was bright as burnished steel and the glare of the sun forced them to use handkerchiefs as makeshift protection for their eyes.

They stopped, exhausted, at noon, and Crowdy made tea while the others rested. They made no move to produce food.

"We'll eat out tonight," Dubuc grunted, as if he made a joke.

Hawker did not trouble to say anything.

They rested three times before it was dark, and each time Crowdy was far in the rear. He sank deeper in the drifts than the others, laboured more in his travelling.

He did not speak as he reached the spot they had chosen for overnight but began building a fire. He filled the kettle with snow and hung it over the flames.

Dubuc sliced more of the bacon carefully and placed it in the pan. Hawker counted the biscuits and his face was grim.

They ate in silence. There was no speech as they gathered fuel or as they slumped on their brush beds, dozing and waking, aching with fatigue. Crowdy had no blankets. The others did not offer to share their bed with him and he dared not ask it. He woke frequently, shivering, and it was he who kept the fire going.

At daylight Hawker issued one biscuit to each after Crowdy had made tea. When they had eaten them and a slim issue of bacon, Dubuc produced a greasy pack of cards.

"We're up ag'in her," he said in a strange, forced tone, looking at Crowdy. "She's five more days anyhow and there's not grub to last. There's only one way to do. We're cuttin' cards and the low man stays out."

Crowdy's heavy features evinced his struggle to gain Dubuc's meaning.

"Stays where?" he asked in bewilderment.

"Out! He's not goin' to have more grub, see."

"Grub?" Crowdy repeated dully. "Why?"

"The low-card man," Dubuc explained with careful, hard

patience, "don' git no more. There ain't enough for t'ree."

Crowdy wet his lips with his tongue.

"But if I draw low I can follow your trail as — as — " He could not finish.

The others nodded.

"We're takin' the same draw," Dubuc said, "I ain't lucky wit' cards. Mebbe it's me. You ready to cut?"

"Wait a minute." Hawker's voice was harsh. "Who said you were running this show?"

Dubuc's black eyes glittered.

"What you want?" he snarled.

"You're not first, and somebody will shuffle for you."

"For you, too," Dubuc flamed. "You git too many aces."

"Is that so!" grated Hawker. "Do you think I was blind back there in the shack when you was slippin' 'em from the bottom?"

"To hell wit' you!" flared Dubuc. "I saw you take discards — twice."

They were each tense with sudden passion. Crowdy, stunned by the turn of events, patted the sack of tea he carried.

"There's plenty of tea," he said. "You ought to let me keep part of it."

The sound of his voice caused the other men to relax.

"Let him cut first." Hawker's voice was thick with suggestion. "An' we'll let him have his share of the tea."

Dubuc shuffled the cards.

"Cut," he said briefly. "Ace is high."

Crowdy had played poker in the shack and had always lost. He pulled off his mitten and cut aimlessly.

"Hell!" Dubuc shouted his amazement. "Look!"

A slow grin widened Crowdy's mouth. He had cut an ace.

"You say who's next." Dubuc pointed at him.

"M-me?" stammered Crowdy. "Why — I'll say you're next."

Hawker seemed to crouch.

"All right," he snarled. "Go ahead."

Dubuc's fingers were cold. He almost dropped the deck in a sliding motion as he split it.

"There she is!" He exhibited another ace.

Hawker jerked off his mittens and reached for the cards, planting the rifle behind him in the snow. He shuffled with lightning speed and the pack seemed to leap apart — at another ace!

"I kin git them same as you," he jeered.

Dubuc's frost-burned face hardened to a terrible intensity. Hawker let the cards fall into the snow and reached for the rifle. He did not move jerkily or with apparent hurry, but with the next heartbeat the weapon was cradled on his arm and he had a bare finger on the trigger. His nostrils dilated and he watched as if he were cornered.

"Wait!" Crowdy shouted, stumbling back from between them. "Don't do anything crazy. Wait. I'll be the one left out. Leave me plenty of tea, that's all."

"Sure," said Dubuc softly, "an' keep the kettle wit' you."

"Yeah," said Hawker, picking up his mittens. "Let's git goin'."

Crowdy stood, staring, as if making a terrific attempt to solve the situation as they climbed from the hollow.

"Wait!" he cried, plunging after them. "Look here. I'm no good at direction and if your tracks get snowed over I'll be lost." He reached inside his jacket. "There's six hundred and fifty dollars in this package. You take it, Dubuc, and mail it when you get out. The address is on it."

"Six hun'erd an' fifty!" Dubuc stared at the thick, sealed packet. "You crazy to have it up here." He placed the packet carefully in his shirt pocket. "I'll look after her mos' sure. Good luck wit' you," he said.

They were ten paces away before Crowdy could find his voice again.

"Good-bye," he called. "I'm going to try to follow you."

Hawker plunged on, headed toward a horizon dotted more thickly with scrub growth. Dubuc looked back once and waved a hand.

They had left Crowdy half the tea. He tied the sack again and tied the small kettle to his belt, then followed the trail in the snow. As he topped the first small rise Hawker's sneering tones came back to him faintly.

" . . . that's how dumb he is, carryin' that much up here."

He kept in their tracks, trying to travel as easily as possible, glancing occasionally at their figures, dark in the distance against the snow dazzle. By noon they were half a mile ahead of him, and when he had made a fire and had plenty of strong tea they were but small specks on the horizon. After a time they vanished altogether.

Crowdy travelled slowly in the loose snow but he maintained his pace. All the afternoon he plodded on, snail-like in the vast solitude. He had lost sight of the others, had stopped trying to see them, but he kept patiently on until it was too dark to travel further. Then he stopped in a hollow and built a fire.

He scooped out snow from beside the fire and made a bed of brush that he broke with his hands. Each move seemed sluggish but he uprooted deadwood with little effort and broke sticks as though they were twigs. He dozed, lying on the brush, waking every once in a while to put fuel on his fire. At midnight he sat up and stared stupidly at the embers. Finally he nodded as if he had reached a decision and filled his kettle with snow. When the tea was ready, he groped in an inner part of his clothing and brought three biscuits to view, then a tin of beans. It was food he had snatched up as he groped for tea in the smoke-filled shack. He had not mentioned having it.

He heated the beans and enjoyed his food, eating slowly and with great relish. The hot drink and the beans drove out the cold that had stabbed his body. He slept easily until the fire died and he shivered again.

At dawn he moved on. He had three more biscuits and he ate them before starting. An hour's travel gave him a wide survey of the region beyond, but no moving dark specks were visible.

The barren gave way to wooded country, spruce in solid rank that made detours necessary. Every now and then a bough would bend suddenly and release its burden of soft snow. The small noises such happenings made and the powdery gusts were ignored. He kept following the trail with the utmost diligence.

Three times during the day he stopped and made tea, and the hot drink ran through him like liquid fire. The scorching flood was at once his food and a supreme luxury. The cold had modified, and the sun had strength in windless places.

At night he made his fire beside some small dead trees. It was easy to get plenty of fuel. There was no wind at all, and the heat of his fire seemed to linger longer. He heaped on the brittle branches and absorbed the soothing warmth. The firelight revealed his rugged features. They were slightly gaunt but there was nothing to suggest that he was tired.

With the first hint of daylight he made tea, and it was still dark in the thickets when he began travelling. Then the bush thinned and presently he was in a long, broad expanse of unspottted whiteness that glittered brilliantly in the morning sun. He had reached the lake.

The tracks he followed led down the centre of it like a straight line and it was noon before he reached the far end. The shore was a steep bank and he toiled in making the ascent. Once up, he went on without a halt and was under the trees when he halted suddenly. For a long moment it was utterly still except for his laboured breathing.

The men whom he was following had made camp under a huge windfall. The brush on which each man had lain was there, bedded in the snow, and he could see the dark yellow stain where they had emptied their tea dregs. But he merely glanced at their camping place. His gaze was fixed on something beyond. It was Dubuc's body, still and distorted, beside the trail!

Crowdy went to it slowly. Twice he halted, aghast, but at last he could see the manner of Dubuc's death. He had been shot through the head!

He stood again before forcing himself to kneel and explore the dead man's clothing. There was no need for fumbling. All the fastenings he had intended undoing were undone. It was easy to reach Dubuc's shirt pocket — but the pocket was empty!

Crowdy surveyed the twisted body in new wonderment as he saw a bullet hole in the jacket, too high up to reach the heart. There had been two shots. He turned, after comprehending, and scanned the tracks. He could see that Dubuc had run several yards before pitching forward.

There were other markings, a zigzag of them. He could see by the different footprints where Hawker had stood, where he had leaped to the left, to right, and where he had fallen sideways and back, as if something had knocked him down. But Hawker was not there now.

Crowdy kicked away snow all around and finally found the axe. Evidently it had felled Hawker and then gone into the drift. Then Crowdy exclaimed aloud. There was blood on the snow. It had dripped freely, the drops were scattered about. Hawker had risen and gone on but he had been hurt.

Crowdy got down and made a patient search of Dubuc's clothing.

"Ah-ah-h!"

He got up and made a fire on the ashes near the windfall. He had made a find. There were seven biscuits and a thick strip of bacon hidden in the lining of Dubuc's jacket.

He ate it all, cutting the bacon with the axe into small bits and gulping it raw, and drinking plenty of hot tea. When he had finished he removed the rolled blanket Dubuc had been carrying and, after a long hesitation, began following Hawker's trail.

At night Crowdy camped in the protection of a thick grove. The weather had warmed considerably and he slept half the night in the warmth of the blanket.

In the morning the sun had such strength that there were melted places on an outcropping of rock that he passed, and snow fell continually from the trees. But he scarcely noticed such signs. He was watching ahead. Hawker's trail was wavering. In the afternoon Crowdy found two places where Hawker had fallen.

Crowdy found Hawker feebly trying to build a fire. He was on his knees in the snow, breaking twigs and feeding them to the flame. Every move he made was slow and uncertain, and he had gathered little fuel beyond the twigs.

"Hello," Crowdy called.

Hawker started so violently he fell backward. He stared

with horror and groped for his rifle. His face was ghastly with fear.

"Hello," Crowdy said again. "Don't you know me?" He had seen where the rifle was sunk in the snow and was between it and Hawker.

"You—you—can't be him!" Hawker gasped. "You—you hadn't anything but tea!"

"It's me all right," said Crowdy. "I had some biscuits in my pockets and a tin of beans."

"In your pockets!" Hawker's bewilderment was on his face. "You?"

"Yes. Me." Crowdy said it with satisfaction. "I know I'm kind of stupid, but I'm telling you the truth. I got them when I was tryin' to find the tea. I saw you weren't going to say anything about that tin of beans you had, so I didn't say anything about what I had. Dubuc had some bacon hid on him, too."

"Dubuc!" Hawker repeated the name hoarsely.

"Yes. I saw where you killed him back there." Crowdy stepped back closer to the rifle in the snow.

"Me!" Hawker tried to shout.

"You," Crowdy said evenly.

"I had to." Hawker looked more ghastly. "He tried to get me with the axe. Look what he did." Hawker pointed to his left shoulder.

The jacket had been slashed. All the clothing was gashed open. Crowdy could see an awkward bandage of torn blanket. It bulged and was soaked with blood.

"He'd have killed me if I hadn't got him," Hawker said. "He was layin' to get me some time and I knowed it." He sank in the snow his length, too weak to remain sitting. "Git some wood," he whined. "I'm freezin' stiff."

Crowdy got some wood, piled it on the fire, and soon had a big blaze going. He got brush for Hawker to lie on. He filled the kettle with snow and began slicing bacon to fry. He had taken Hawker's sack of food without asking permission.

Hawker lay back on the brush, watching. He drank the hot tea and ate a little food, then shook his head.

"She's hurtin' bad," he said. "Too much."

Crowdy made a bigger fire. He had eaten most of the bacon and many biscuits and he felt better. He opened Hawker's jacket and examined the wound. It was a frightful hurt. The axe had bitten deep and blood oozed continually. Hawker's clothing was sodden with it.

"Does it — look bad?" Hawker asked.

"Very bad," said Crowdy. He arranged the pad as best he could, and stood up. "I don't know what to do," he said.

"It's two days more to outside." Hawker's voice held no hope. "I can't make it. I — I guess I'm done." It seemed an increasing effort for him to talk.

"It's too bad," Crowdy said. He was bewildered. "Would you like more tea?"

"Yes," Hawker said. "It warms me. I never knowed it could be so cold."

"It's because you're hurt." Crowdy filled the kettle again. "It ain't really cold."

Hawker settled back on the brush. "Then I guess I'm goin' to pass out," he said, his voice little more than a whisper.

"You tell me anything I can do," said Crowdy. He put more wood on the fire and tucked both blankets around Hawker.

"You got — paper — and pencil?"

"Sure." Crowdy produced a small notebook. "I was keepin' account of what fur I took," he said.

"Quick — while I'm settin' up," Hawker panted. He wrote in a hand that scrawled over two pages.

"I killed Jen Dubuc. I shot him to git what he carried. He got me with the axe. I'm ritin this so you won't blame anybody else. Sim Hawker."

"There." Hawker slumped back on the brush. "Give that to Tom Jerry. He's the policeman at the Cove. Or constable. He — knows — my writin'. That'll — clear — you."

"Thanks," Crowdy said. "That's mighty good of you."

"No — it ain't." Hawker rolled his head on the brush. "Me'n — him — left — you — dirty. We should — have — stuck — together. You — you're — white."

"I might have kept up," Crowdy said. "I wish you'd told

Dubuc it was you fixed the fire that night. He blamed it on me.''

Hawker made no response. It was a long time before he spoke. "Listen—the river's—just ahead. Keep—to—the—bank—this side. It'll—take—you—in.''

It was very dark and the light of the fire danced and wavered along the trees. Crowdy stood beside Hawker but he did not know what he should do.

"It's—here.'' Hawker tried to get a hand in his pocket but was too weak. Crowdy bent over and helped him. It was the packet he had given Dubuc. Hawker tried to speak again but failed.

Crowdy saw him stiffen and knew he was dead. He gathered more wood for the fire, then knelt beside Hawker and searched his pockets. He found six biscuits and a tin of beans.

The hollow where he had made the fire was a small depression and there was not room enough to make another brush bed. Crowdy stood and after a long hesitation dragged the dead man to a spot outside the circle of light. Then he rearranged the brush bed and renewed the fire.

He sat a time, staring into the flames, frowning in heavy concentration, then drew the sealed packet from his pocket. After more deliberation he tore it open, revealing a weasel skin and a letter.

"Dear Aunt Amy,'' he read. "I promised I'd send you the first skin I caught, and here it is. It's a good one. I hope you are satisfied now that I can be a trapper.''

"If I hadn't had that to mail,'' Crowdy muttered, "I wouldn't have had anything I could have fooled them with.'' He tossed the fur, wrapping, and letter on the fire. "You wouldn't have thought fellows like them would have swallowed what I told them,'' he went on, as if arguing with himself. "It's a mighty lucky thing for me I thought quick enough to try it.'' He gazed into the darkness where he had dragged Hawker. "They'd do anything, them two,'' he said loudly, as if defying the dark.

Then he reached for the kettle. He had decided he would

eat the tin of beans before he slept.

It was growing dark two days later when he reached Angel Cove. He went to the door where his Aunt Amy lived and rapped. She opened it and stared at him.

"We've been wonderin' how you were gettin' on," she said. "Come right in. We've had our supper but I'll whip up some fried potatoes and cod in no time. Where's your fur?"

"We had bad luck," said Crowdy. "We were in a shack the pulpwood men had and it took on fire one night and we just managed to git out ourselves. We didn't have time to save one skin."

"Dear glory," said his aunt. "You do have bad luck. Where'd the other two go?"

"They didn't git back," said Crowdy. "They walked faster'n me and I was away back. They had a row and killed each other. Well, almost. One was still alive when I caught up but he'd been cut terrible with an axe."

"Pink codfish!" exclaimed Aunt Amy. "Don't you go talkin' about it. We've got a good name in the Cove."

"But what'll I tell Aunt Mary? I'm sure to meet her sometime and you know what she's like."

"Tell her they went ahead of you and you had to come out by yourself. Don't say any more than that."

Jim Crowdy stayed in the house for three days, then it was such fine weather he could not stay longer. Everyone was busy with their boats, for the ice was going, and no one bothered him. Then he met a stranger who was wearing a nice blue suit and looked prosperous. "I stopped overnight with Mrs. Pertwee," he said. "I guess you call her Aunt Mary. I'm from the St. John's paper and I'm looking for some stories. She said you'd been away some time on a trapping trip. Did anything much happen?"

"No," said Crowdy, twisting uneasily. "Just a lot of trampin'. But Tom Holder lives across the road there and he was on a schooner that passed right close to a polar bear on some ice."

"Thanks ever so much," said the newspaper man. "We like any kind of adventure story. I'll go and see him."

Triangle in Steel

Thomas H. Raddall

They were sitting on the mangled earth of the river bank, looking across the shining stream to the edge of the woods where the steel bones of the new railway bridge came to rest. The reporter had the story of that new bridge in his notebook; the tons of cement, of sand, of aggregate, of steel; the millions of feet of timber, yes, even the gallons of paint that would cover it when the job was done.

He had the number of men employed, and the impressive total of their wages. He knew just what stresses the big girders would carry when the train finally rolled across, and he had to a decimal of an inch the contraction that would take place in that rigid metal skeleton between the heat of this summer day and a winter temperature of twenty below zero.

He had several pages of proof that the new bridge was secure against flood and ice when the river broke up in spring, for that had been the downfall of the old one. His head reeled and his notebook bristled with figures — wind pressure and deformation stress and dead load and live load, and the impact of live load plus speed. And he was bored stiff. So was the Assistant Superintendent of Construction, who had been told to usher the reporter over the job and see that the Archimedes Construction Company had prominent mention in the account.

A cool breeze came down the river in little gusts, and with its uncertain breath the tac-tac-tac of riveting hammers now purred faintly and now rattled with the sudden violence of machine-gun fire.

"Those riveters," the reporter said. "Look here, there's something odd about those riveters."

"French-Canadians?" murmured the Assistant Superintendent. "They're all right. What's odd about them?"

"Well, some of 'em are very dark. There's a certain set of the eyes and cheek bones."

"Those are Indians."

"What?"

"Why not? The Caughnawagas have their reservation right alongside a big structural steel plant and they've learned the trade. What's strange about that?"

"Well, after all, the red man's supposed to be incapable of learning a skilled trade; and there he is, crawling like a fly in that spider's web of steel, and handling a pneumatic hammer as if born to it."

"Yes, and getting a dollar or two an hour, while plenty of the more or less lordly whites are mucking away with a pick and shovel at forty cents an hour, and glad to get it. When you see a structural steel worker with a sunburn that doesn't wear off, anywhere between the Soo and the sea, ten to one he's a Caughnawaga and a darned good man."

"Makes you think, doesn't it?"

"Think what?"

"Put the Indian next to white man's business and make a white man of him."

"You can't do that — an Indian's an Indian."

"But — a dollar an hour!"

"Makes no difference."

Listen! (the A.S. went on.) Fifteen years ago I had a job at Michekanni Falls. That's how I fell in with the Archimedes people; they'd got a contract to build a big paper mill in the bush, and I was sent up there to represent the architect. I lived in a drafty barrack of pine boards and tar paper with the rest of the construction staff, but I had a small office of my own, a shack in the midst of the job, with a chair, a pine desk and a telephone. There were blueprints tacked all over the walls and stuffed under the desk — enough to sink a ship — and more arriving in every mail.

In six months I had the blues — environment, you might say. I was city-bred and I was young. I'd looked forward to this job at Michekanni as an adventure in the wilds, not to mention being my own boss for a time, but after a time the novelty went out of it, and I was far from being my own boss. The architect was no further away than the end of a telegraph wire, which he kept humming with instructions.

The construction company's telegraph bill averaged five hundred dollars a month, and most of it had to do with the deep blue sea of plans that beat up around me and threatened to drown me and cut me off from everything — you know, like Robinson Crusoe.

The steel frame of the mill was sprouting from the bedrock by the river, with the camp, all grey tarred-felt shacks and tin chimney-pipes, on the slope behind, and the railway running off into the woods as straight as a rifle barrel. When you stood on the track it led your eye towards the horizon through that narrow corridor in the bush, until the rails came together with a final glitter in the distance like the farewell wave of a hand. You felt as if you were a thousand miles from anywhere.

Actually there was a town of sorts not forty miles down the line, a cluster of unpainted wooden houses, a bank and a church and a barber's shop, all squatting around a bankrupt lumber mill like crows about a corpse.

It wasn't long before the camp began to find its way over there. A bootlegger appeared; then a flock of bootleggers. When a construction worker hits town after a week in the bush there are two things he wants. Liquor's one. Well, demand created supply. That little dead settlement came to life with a bang. We had nine hundred men in camp and the payroll was never less than thirty thousand dollars a week — often more.

Personally I preferred the camp, noisy and dirty as it was. And to get away from the monotony of grey huts and blue-prints I went for walks in the woods. One day I discovered the Indians. Steel workers. They wouldn't live in the grey barracks like the rest of us, but brought their women and children over the railway and stuck up queer little shacks in the bush a quarter-mile from the job. A dozen or fifteen huts, wigwams — whatever you want to call 'em — made of poles and boards swiped from the concrete forms, with the ce-ment still crusted on 'em, with a covering of burlap bags and bits of roofing felt, and brushwood and sheets of birch bark, and a lot of those indestructible paper sacks the cement companies use, all slung together anyhow.

They looked as if a stiff breeze would blow 'em all away, but the spot was chosen for shelter, a gully in the hillside, shut in by spruce and fir and birch, with a clear spring trickling out of the ledge rock under a poplar tree. A snug place. You might hunt the bush for a month to find such a place. Those Indians had gone to it by instinct. What else? They'd lived on the edge of a big city for generations, spoke French, yes, and read and wrote French, and had a pretty fair smattering of English besides; and they'd been earning big money all their adult lives, on construction jobs mostly in cities, and they knew the world of shops and cars and theatres as well as we do; but they had that ancient instinct for seclusion, for shelter, and knew how to find it.

I can't say they welcomed me, the stranger, the white-collar man, the intruder from the womanless camp below; but they were polite, and I sat on a log beside one of the huts, with the men squatting about me, and we talked. It was no great effort. The kids were friendly; we got along very well. I was able to do small favors for the men, in the way of banking their pay and so on, and after a few visits they thawed.

We had fine talks in that hidden camp on the hillside.

They were intelligent and good humored, they'd been all over the Dominion and used their eyes and ears, and they had the Indian love of a tale. I came to know their names, and when you can hail people by name, with the exact pronunciation, without fail, you're practically in the family bosom.

The men were in the twenties and early thirties—you have to be young in the steel game—and when in the hot summer evenings they went down to the river and stripped for a bathe, you found yourself looking at a Greek frieze. They were lean and beautifully muscled from head to foot. Steel work does that for a man, where you have to hang on with your legs to some dizzy perch while you work very hard with your arms. Their knees and ankles were callused from eternal shinning up and down the vertical steel, and from hanging on to the horizontals.

And steel work did something else for them; it had given those stolid Caughnawagas an air of potential activity, a ready-for-anything manner, like sailors.

I liked to watch them at work. You know how steel goes up? The erectors come first, slinging the posts and girders and trusses and braces into place with their cranes, and fixing them true with bolts and nuts. That's all blueprint work. I watched it like a mother at a christening. Then the riveters come along, taking the bolts out and hammering rivets in their place.

Of all the riveting gangs the Indians were the best. It was fine to watch 'em—as good as a ball game. Teams of four, you know; riveter, sticker, and bucker-up perching themselves on a girder, and the heater with his little portable forge somewhere below, on the nearest solid footing he can find.

The best team was a dark-skinned quartet named Napoléon, Onésime, Grégoire, and just plain John. John was the heater. He'd pick a red-hot rivet out of the coals with his tongs and give it a long underarm swing, opening the tongs at the end of the arc with a precision that took your breath, and the rivet went sailing up, up, straight as a bullet to the sticker waiting on the girder above. And the sticker — that was Onésime—sat there with his little tin pail in one hand, cool as ice, while the rivet came at him; and not more than twenty inches from his brown beak nose he'd make a swift pass at the thing, a scooping gesture from right to left, and—tang!—there was the hot rivet in the bucket. He'd pick it out with his tongs and slip it into place in the steel.

Then Grégoire'd shove his heavy bucking-iron against the rivet's head while 'Poléon on the other side battered the glowing end with his pneumatic hammer—rat-a-tat-tat!—working the hammer with a circular motion as the hot metal squeezed down, "rolling it" as we say, until there was another perfect head, round and even-shouldered like the one on the other end. We had some good men but no one could roll a head like 'Poléon. It was an art.

It was more; when you consider those men hanging over the edge of nothing, holding on by the grip of their knees, working both arms, shoving with all their might on bucking-iron and hammer, with the hammer-blows shaking them like a fit of the palsy, and maybe a stiff wind blowing down the river and whistling through the high steel. I tell you it was a feat as good as anything you'd see in a circus. And not performed for a few dramatic minutes to the roll of drums, with the ringmaster pointing a theatrical white-gloved finger, but carried on, "Comin' up!—*tang!*—*rat-tat-tat* " for ten hours on end, and nobody caring a hoot.

These four I came to know well. 'Poléon was unmarried. His sister, a squat solemn woman, was the wife of Grégoire, and 'Poléon lived in their hut. Onésime had a wife as like Mrs. Grégoire as one brown frog is like another, and two small black-eyed boys. John was the oldest of the four, active and muscular as any, but a little fat, a little past his prime. You could see that John would never be anything but a heater, would never hold Grégoire's heavy bucking-iron, would never be able to boast, like 'Poléon, of the rivets he could drive in a ten-hour day.

But he was a good heater. I've seen John toss a hot rivet sixty-five feet straight to the mark, and Onésime catching it in the shallow tin bucket with the superb and careless skill that comes of long practice and complete confidence in the heater's throw. And in the camp in the woods John could boast what 'Poléon could not, nor Grégoire, nor Onésime for that matter — a young and handsome wife.

She could not have been more than eighteen, for those women get fat early and she was as slim as a sapling birch. She had the long oval face and pointed chin, the strong cheekbones and wide-set eyes of her people. Her eyes were lively and black—black as her shining hair—and she carried herself with the erect grace bequeathed her by untold squaws carrying infants strapped to their backs.

The other Indian women dressed like their men, in blue denim overalls and grey flannel shirts, with a cast-off cap or an old felt hat of their husband's, and a pair of their husband's old boots as like as not. You could spot a steel worker's boots at a glance—grooved up the inner sides from just before the heel to a point near the swell of the ankle-bone, from sliding down I-beams, with heels hooked on the flanges, whenever the whistle blew.

But none of that for Madeleine! She wore skirts always, and silk stockings that showed more than they covered of her slim strong legs. It was ridiculous in that hole in the bush, where there was no one to see and admire. But there was something pathetic about it. You could sense her longing to be home, in the glimmer of city lights, where a young wife could parade her finery before the world. What was the good of earning all this money, of living in this primitive economy for months on end, if you couldn't make some display of the earnings and savings?

The other steel workers respected the Indians for their skill but despised them otherwise. I used to think it was jealousy—after all it's not edifying to be beaten at your own game by what your white egoism has always considered an inferior race. But I came to know that it was the Indians' frugality that made them contemptible in the eyes of the camp. The steel workers were gorgeous spendthrifts, the finest in camp, and that made the little Indian group seem all the more miserly.

When the steel gang went down the line for a week-end spree in Timberton, the bootleggers rubbed their hands and got out their most poisonous stock, and the town constable took to the woods. I've said the steel men despised the Indians; that's too sweeping, there was an exception. They liked 'Poléon. 'Poléon was one of the boys. 'Poléon went to town and whooped it up with the best of 'em. He could drink that Timberton rot-gut hour after hour and keep charge of his hands and feet, and never got nasty as Indians in liquor are said to do; though when it came to a fight, 'Poléon would fight with gusto.

And he could sit in that blood-curdling poker game in the big room over Merton's bowling alley, where the sky was the limit and money poured across the table like water, and draw and bluff and ante-up with a hand that never shook, a grin that never wavered. And he laughed and roared the bawdy songs of the camp, and bragged of the rivets he could drive in a day, of the money he earned in a week and spent in a week-end, of the girls he had loved in "Mo'real" and other points east and west.

Suddenly, in September, in the long fine days between summer and fall, with the maples turning color and the river flowing thinly after the summer's drought, with the northern lights making their first experimental flickers in the evening sky, 'Poléon stopped going to town. He lay about the little Indian camp for days at a time, sending excuses down to the steel boss by John or Grégoire.

"'Poléon," John would explain in his charming English, "he don't feel pritty good."

On these days Grégoire took over the hammer job and the boss sent up a young French-Canadian to hold the bucking-iron. He was a good man but somehow the team didn't work as well. Even John fell off, the steady unerring John, and frequently a rivet went wild, beyond Onésime's reach.

Now a red-hot rivet falling fifty or a hundred feet is an uncomforatble thing to the men below. The ground crew swore up into the air, and complained to the erector fore-man, and the foreman spoke to John.

"Keep your mind on your work," he suggested.

John shrugged. The ground crew took to watching. When 'Poléon was on the job, all went well; when 'Poléon was absent, they kept a wary eye on John and his rivets. The bricklayers didn't mind. They were directly below but the wild rivets always went outward.

It was tough on the blasting crew, the steam shovel men, the jack-hammer men and the gang of muckers. They were grading what was supposed to be the mill yard, and there was a big reef of exposed bedrock to be shattered and picked and shovelled and trucked away. At the cry of "Heads, there!" they had to scuttle to safety over a jumble of broken rock, and they didn't like it — who would? The ground foreman cussed and talked darkly of helmets, but the construction boss grunted at that and said it was easier to hire a heater who could throw.

One day when 'Poléon was absent on one of his frequent "spells", John tossed a rivet clear of Onésime's bucket, clear of everything, and it came down in a beautiful arc to the roof of the temporary oil store, a tar-paper shack like the rest of the camp. Nobody saw where it landed till smoke began to curl up from the roof, and there was a mighty scurry for fire buckets. There was no great damage but it gave the construction boss a scare, and he got the crane operator to sling him up onto the steel where John's little forge was glowing. He told John a number of things in a wrapping of really brilliant profanity and at the end he said:

"Another one like that, fella, an' you're fired. It's a hard game, the steel, an' if you're gettin' past it, why, say so, an' I'll get another man now."

"I'm all ri'," protested John quietly. "Eet's 'Poléon, boss, 'Poléon ain' 'ere, I'm no good. 'Poléon 'ere, I'm all ri'."

That touched another sore spot. "'Poléon!" snapped the boss. "Is 'Poléon the only riveter on this job? I'll fire 'Poléon too if he don't show up more reg'lar. Lazy, that's what's wrong with 'Poléon. I won't stand for any o' this on-again-off-again stuff on a job o' mine — mind what I say! I'm a patient man but I'm no Injun's uncle an' you an' 'Poléon'll find that out!"

I missed this affair because that afternoon I knocked off for a stroll in the bush, away from that bedlam of jack-hammers and riveting hammers and steam shovels and cranes and hoists. They'd set up an air compressor outside my shack, one of those gasoline things that roar and then whisper, in irregular periods, hour after hour, and it was slowly driving me mad.

I didn't visit the Indians—I never went up there when the men weren't present. Besides, a change had come over that little rustic paradise. The quiet was still there, and the shade, and the kids playing on the bare earth by the spring. But the people were different. They talked to me in an odd way, as if they were thinking of somebody else, and there was a tense-ness about them as if they were all waiting for something to happen — something that was none of my business. So I walked by the river. The maples shut off all sight of the job, the grey squalor of the camp and the brick walls of the new mill rising out of it like a great pink monument to Mammon.

About a mile above, where a strip of wild meadow came out of the trees to the river, I heard the voice of a man and a girl. The girl's first, singing something in a low husky voice, rather pleasing. It was *A la Claire Fontaine*. You know how it goes —

> *A la claire fontaine*
> *M'en allant promener . . .*

The tune ended abruptly, and I heard the man's voice, low and urgent. I halted then, in a clump of alders. They were sitting in the wild grass under the gnarled trunk of an old maple, and making love; or perhaps I should say 'Poléon was making love and Madeleine taking it, greedily. The bobbed hair, black and smooth and faintly iridescent like the folded wings of a grackle, hung down as her head went back and back under the rain of his kisses, a black and shining mop.

And between the kisses she laughed softly, a queer cooing sound. A disturbing sound — I was young then. But I was shocked. I was no prude, you understand. After all, I'd lived six months in the atmosphere of the camp. I can't explain it exactly. I respected those Indian people. They'd discovered how to earn the white man's money in big chunks, but they weren't letting it drag them down to his frantic way of life. I liked that. They were sane, sane, and all the rest of us were lunatics. And now — well, it was as if you'd walked into a garden and caught a whiff of offal amongst the flowers. I went away in a stealthy rush.

Next day 'Poléon was back on the job, and the team as usual went like clockwork. I went up on the steel in the morning because the erector foreman claimed something wrong with the blueprints, and I knew quite well it was nothing more than a piece of steel wrongly marked. It was the framework of the mill's chip loft, the topmost part of the main building, and the riveting gangs were hard on the heels of the erector crew, with the bricklayers coming a bad third. From where I stood I could look down at John busily turning the bellows crank of his smoking forge, and up at 'Poléon and Onésime and Grégoire sitting astride a girder on the edge of the framework.

They were in good form; it was an easy toss for John, thirty feet perhaps, and the rivets went up straight as bullets to Onésime's little bucket, and the chatter of 'Poléon's hammer rose triumphantly above the noise of the job. Have you ever heard a yellow-flicker on a camp roof, setting up a tattoo on the tin chimney, not because he thinks there's a worm inside but for the sheer joy of it, for the lovely rolling sound of it? It was like that — 'Poléon's hammer.

The erector boss said, "Jiminy! Those Indians are *on* to-day. If they keep it up they'll have a new day's record." And he turned to the blueprints, aware that all this demanded more speed from his bolting crew. We got the tangle straightened out — a truss incorrectly marked — and I stood there for a time, one arm around an I-beam, looking over the ant-heap of the works.

It was a grey day, with a threat of rain in a wind that blew in a fidgety way up the river, ruffling the trees like a squall on the sea, and bending the various smokes of the camp and job in long ragged wisps against the earth. The river ran cleanly — soon to be poisoned by waste sulphite liquor and pulp screenings—and on the far side stretched the forest that was doomed by our coming. Below, the toy steam shovels rattled and puffed, and toy trucks lurched away with loads of grey rock, and human ants swarmed in the debris of the shattered outcrop.

My eyes wandered back to 'Poléon and his riveting team. I watched John whip a glowing rivet out of the coals, watched the smooth swing of the tongs, the release at the end of it, the rivet sailing up. John stood posed like a golfer at the end of his swing, a statue in bronze, arm outstretched, tongs rigidly pointed, watching the rivet's flight as a golfer watches the driven ball. Then the swift pass of Onésime's hand and the tin bucket crying *tang* ! and the lightning transfer from bucket to bolt hole, the rivet glowing still but a duller red, and a little ripple of yellow sparks flittering over it as it entered the cold steel of the beam; and the slam of Grégoire's bucking-iron against the head of it, and 'Poléon leaning out over the abyss, held by the crook of a knee and the thrust of a toe, shoving the hammer hard on the rivet end, and the hammer's harsh song rising once more.

I don't know what made me look down at John then. He was whipping another rivet out of the forge, stepping clear for the swing. I glanced up quickly. 'Poléon was beginning to roll the head, with Grégoire bearing hard on the bucking-iron and Onésime crouched on the girder beside them, watching the rolling of the head, as he always did. I looked down again, puzzled. They were not ready for another rivet. But I saw the swing of John's tongs, saw them open, saw the bright red rivet flying upward, saw John poised for a moment in the intent follow-through — and saw him break the pose sharply and busy himself with the forge. All this in seconds.

The rivet took 'Poléon full in the face. He uttered a cry, not very loud, a sharp "Ha!" and threw up his hands. He seemed to launch himself into space like a diver into a pool, with his legs rigid and together but with his hands clutched to his face. He floated downward slowly — it was incredible how slowly—as if he cared no more for the law of gravity than the law of man and wife. Far down he flung out his arms as a bird launched from the nest puts out its wings; but 'Poléon had no wings, and it was ninety feet to the blasted rocks in the yard below. Beyond that first exclamation of agonized surprise he uttered no sound.

When the delayed thud of his fall came up to me, it was followed by a confusion of shouts from the mucker gang, and the human ants swarmed. One after another the sounds of machinery halted until there was a vast and awful silence. You could have heard a nail drop anywhere on the job. I wanted to go down at once, but my knees were knocking and I had to wait. Above me Grégoire and Onésime sat astride the girder, staring at each other. Then slowly they turned their faces down — down to John, at his little forge.

And he looked up at them, a long inscrutable gaze. Behind those three brown masks you sensed something terrible and old, the satisfaction of a primitive rite, a giving of account, a pondering and a vote of confidence, all in the awful flood of silence that welled up from the ground and drowned us and went on to the sky.

And then John made a curious gesture, a stroke of the clenched hand in air, and you had a queer feeling you'd seen it before, in some other existence, long ago; but there was something missing and you couldn't, for the life of you, think what it was. And then you knew; you missed the haft of the tomahawk in the fist.

'Poléon was beyond recognition when they picked him up. He'd fallen face down. They took the body to Timberton's coroner on a work train. Grégoire was the only witness. 'Poléon had been hitting the booze too much, he said. 'Poléon had been sleeping it off, two or three days at a time, for weeks. Today he must have taken a fit — he fumbled for the exact English word, and failing said *"le vertige"*. That was all he knew and it satisfied the jury. The inquest rendered a verdict of death by accident, and with the usual pomposity recommended that some sort of net be suspended beneath the riveting gangs — a joke in the camp for months.

But I don't need to say any more. There it is, there's my point! The primitive justice of the thing — considered, measured, delivered, and no questions asked. …

"But you can't leave the story there!" protested the reporter. "What happened to Madeleine?"

"Ah, you newspaper fellows are so darned objective. Why should there be any more? Proved my point, haven't I? How should I know what happened to Madeleine? I never went up to the gully again. Something told me they weren't receiving visitors any more. I can fancy Grégoire and Onésime walking back to their huts that day and announcing 'Poléon's dramatic exit from life in a few grunted words. And I can fancy them all standing silent, and John and Madeleine staring at each other the way John and Grégoire and Onésime had stared, up there on the steel — the question, the answer, the stolid acceptance, and the seal of an ancient code over all, a code going back to a time — who knows? — when the whites themselves dressed in skins and swung the early European counterpart of a tomahawk.

"Grégoire took over 'Poléon's riveting hammer and Onésime got the reward of his long and patient study — the job of bucker-up. They put a nephew of Grégoire's on as sticker. John? John kept tossing rivets, with never a miss. At the job's end they came out of the woods and vanished over the railway, just as they'd come. Mysterious. Mysterious. A separate creation, I tell you.

"Look there — you see that new bridge, don't you? It fills the eye. When you stand at this spot you can't see anything else. But look—there's the river, old as the face of the earth. It flows out of the woods, it passes quietly under that gleaming metal thing and disappears into the woods again. When you and I are dead and forgotten; when this bridge is gone like the one before it, and gone forever because somehow there's no need of rails and bridges any more—that river will still be flowing out of the woods and past the ruin and into the woods again."

"Like the spirit of John, I suppose!"

"And Madeleine — and 'Poléon."

"And Grégoire?"

"Grégoire of course! There must always be someone to

covet 'Poléon's job, to bide his time, to drop the inflaming word, and see the ends of justice served. Always a Grégoire to profit by the sins of others. That's where the red man's code joins with ours. From there we march together.''

Hurry, Hurry

Ethel Wilson

When the mountains beyond the city are covered with snow to their base, the late afternoon light falling obliquely from the west upon the long slopes discloses new contours. For a few moments of time the austerity vanishes, and the mountains appear innocently folded in furry white. Their daily look has gone. For these few moments the slanting rays curiously discover each separate tree behind each separate tree in the infinite white forests. Then the light fades, and the familiar mountains resume their daily look again. The light has gone, but those who have seen it will remember.

As Miriam stood at the far point of Sea Island, with the wind blowing in from the west, she looked back towards the city. There was a high ground fog at the base of the mountains, and so the white flanks and peaks seemed to lie unsupported in the clear spring sky. They seemed to be unattached to the earth. She wished that Allan were with her to see this sight of beauty which passed even as she looked upon it. But Allen was away, and she had come for a walk upon the dyke alone with their dogs.

It was the very day in spring that the soldier blackbirds had returned from Mexico to the marshes of the delta. Just a few had come, but in the stubble fields behind the high dyke, and in the salt marshes seawards from the dyke, and on the shallow sea, and over the sea there were thousands of other birds. No people anywhere. Just birds. The salt wind blew softly from the sea, and the two terrier dogs ran this way and that, with and against the wind. A multitude of little sandpipers ran along the wet sands as if they were on wheels. They whispered and whimpered together as they ran, stabbing with their long bills into the wet sands and running on. There was a continuous small noise of birds in the air. The terriers bore down upon the little sandpipers. The terriers ran clumsily, sinking in the marshy blackish sand, encumbered as they ran and the little sandpipers rose and flew low together to a safer sandbank. They whispered and wept together as they fled in a cloud, animated by one enfolding spirit of motion. They settled on their safe sandbank, running and jabbing the wet sand with their bills. The terriers like little earnest monsters bore down upon them again in futile chase, and again the whispering cloud of birds arose. Miriam laughed at the silly hopeful dogs.

Farther out to sea were the duck and the brant and the seagulls. These strutted on the marsh-like sands, or lay upon the shallow water or flew idly above the water. Sometimes a great solitary heron arose from nowhere and flapped across the wet shore. The melancholy heron settled itself in a motionless hump, and again took its place in obscurity among stakes and rushes.

Behind the dyke where Miriam stood looking out to sea was a steep bank sloping to a shallow salt-water ditch, and beyond that again, inland, lay the stubble fields of Sea Island, crossed by rough hedges. From the fields arose the first song of the meadow lark, just one lark, how curious after winter to hear its authentic song again. Thousands of ducks showed themselves from the stubble fields, rising and flying without haste or fear to the sea.

Miriam called to the dogs and walked on along the narrow clay path at the top of the dyke. She delighted in the birds and the breeze and the featureless ocean. The dogs raced after her.

Clumps of bare twisted bushes were scattered along the edge of the path, sometimes obscuring the curving line of the dyke ahead. In a bush a few early soldier blackbirds talked to each other. Miriam stood still to listen. "Oh-kee-*ree*," called a blackbird. "Oh-kee-*ree*," answered his mate. "Oh-kee-*ree*," he said. "Oh-kee-*ree*," she answered. Then the male bird flew. His red patches shone finely. What a strange note, thought Miriam, there's something sweet and something very ugly. The soldier blackbird's cry began on a clear flute's note and ended in piercing sweetness. The middle sound grated like a rusty lock. As she walked on between the twisted black bushes more soldier blackbirds called and flew. Oh-kee-*ree*! Oh-kee-*ree*! Sweet and very ugly.

Suddenly she saw a strange object. Below her on the left, at the edge of the salt-water ditch there was an unlikely heap of something. Miriam stopped and looked. This thing was about the size of a tremendous hunched cat, amorphous, of a rich reddish brown. It was the rich brown of a lump of rotted wood. Although it did not move, she had instant warning that this creature was alive and had some meaning for her. She called the dogs who came wagging. She leashed them, and they went forward together. The dogs tugged and tugged. Soon they too looked down the bank at the strange object. In the brown mass something now moved. Miriam saw that the brown object was a large wounded hawk. The hawk was intensely aware of the woman and the dogs. As they paused, and then as they passed along the high dyke path, the hawk's head turned slowly, very slowly, to observe them. Its body was motionless. Its eyes were bright with comprehension. Miriam was glad that she had leashed the dogs. In another minute they would have descended on the hawk. One brown wing lay trailed behind the big bird, but with its sharp beak and tearing claws it would have mauled the terriers, and they would have tormented it. The hawk stared brightly at her. She wished that she could save the hawk from its lingering death on the marshes, but there was nothing she could do. Motionless, save for the slowly turning head, the great bird followed them with intent gaze. Its eyes were bright with comprehension, but no fear. It was ready. The hawk made Miriam feel uneasy. She walked on faster, keeping the dogs still on the leash. She looked back. The hawk steadily watched her. She turned and walked on still faster.

One of the dogs growled and then both barked loudly. Round a thorn bush, hurrying towards her came a man. In all their walks upon the dyke before Allan went away, they had never met another human being. Miriam was startled. She was almost afraid. The strange hawk. The strange man. The man stopped. He was startled too. Then he hurried towards her. Crowded on the narrow clayey path of the dyke stood Miriam and the two dogs, uncertain. The man came close to her and stopped.

"Don't go on," he said urgently, "don't go on. It isn't safe. There's a cougar. I'm going to a farmhouse. To warn them. Perhaps I can get a gun. Turn back. And keep your dogs on the lead," he said sharply.

"Oh," said Miriam, "you must be mistaken. There's never been a cougar on these islands. No, of course I won't go on though. I'll turn back at once. But you *must* be mistaken. A dog or even a coyote, but not a cougar!"

"It *is* a cougar," said the man vehemently. "Did you never hear of the cougar that swam across from the North Shore last year? Well — I can't stop to argue — there *is* a cougar, I saw it. Beside the dyke. It's driven in by hunger, starving, I expect. Well?"

He looked at her. He held her eyes with his eyes.

"Oh," said Miriam, "of course I won't go on. I should never have come! I'm so glad I met you. But it's extraordinary!" and she turned in haste.

The man paid her no further attention. He stepped down a bit from the path on to the steep grassy side of the dyke, and pushed past her and the restless dogs. He walked on very fast without another word. Miriam hurried after him along the narrow dyke path, the dogs impeding her as she hurried. This was like a bad dream. Hurry, hurry! I can't hurry.

She nearly ran along the slippery bumpy dyke path, past the brown heap of the wounded hawk whose bright eyes watched her, and past the straggly bushes where the soldier blackbirds flew from tree to tree and sang. She hurried along until she turned the curve of the dyke and saw again the mountains behind the city. The peaks now hung pink and gold in the cold spring sky. To the farthest range of the Golden Ears the sunset caught them. Miriam fled on. The leashed dogs ran too, bounding and hindering her as she ran. She crossed the little footbridge that led to the lane that led to her car.

She had lost sight of the man a long time ago. He had hurried on to give the alarm. She had seen him stumbling down the steep dyke side and splashing across the salt-water ditch to the stubble fields.

Far behind them along the dyke the body of the young woman who had just been murdered lay humped beside the salt-water ditch.

The man who had killed her reached the cover of the hedge, out of sight of that woman with the dogs. When he reached the cover of the hedge he began to run across the tussocky field, stumbling, half blind, sobbing, crying out loud.

The
Firing Squad

Colin McDougall

He was the first Canadian soldier sentenced to death, and rear headquarters in Italy seethed with the prospect of carrying it out. At his marble-topped desk in Rome Major-General Paul Vincent read the instructions from London with distaste. The findings of the court martial had been confirmed by Ottawa — that meant by a special session of the cabinet, the General supposed — and it was now the direct responsibility of the Area Commander that the execution of Private Sydney Jones should be proceeded with "as expeditiously as possible".

The hum of voices and the quick beat of teletypes in the outer office marked the measure of Rome's agitation. No one had expected this confirmation of sentence. Not even the officers who had sentenced Private Jones to death. For them, indeed, there had been little choice; Jones had even wanted to plead guilty, but the court had automatically changed his plea, and gone on to record its inevitable finding and sentence.

The salient facts of the case filed quickly through the neat corridors of General Vincent's mind. This Jones, a young soldier of twenty-two, had deserted his unit, had joined with a group of deserter-gangsters who operated in Rome and Naples, and had been present when his companions shot and killed a U.S. military policeman. All this Jones admitted, and the court could pass no other sentence. The execution of a Canadian soldier, however, was more than a military matter: it touched on public policy; and higher authorities had never before confirmed a sentence of death. But now the confirming order was in his hands and the train of events must be set in motion.

General Vincent sighed. He preferred to think of himself as the business executive he happened to be rather than a general officer whose duty it was to order a man's death. An execution was something alien and infinitely distasteful. Well, if this thing had to be done under his command at least it need not take place under his personal orders. From the beginning he had known just the man for the job. Already the teletype had clicked off its command to Volpone, the reinforcement base where Private Jones was imprisoned, and a staff car would now be rushing the commander of that base, Brigadier Benny Hatfield, to Rome. The General sighed again and turned to some more congenial correspondence on his desk.

A dirt track spiraled out of Volpone and mounted in white gashes upon the forested mountain side. Fifty infantry reinforcements, fresh from Canada, were spaced along the first two miles of zigzag road. They carried all the paraphernalia of their fledgling trade: rifles, machine guns, and light mortars. Some were trying to run, lurching ahead with painful steps; others stopped to stand panting in their own small lakes of sweat. One or two lay at the roadside, faces turned from the sun, awaiting the stabbing scorn of their sergeant with spent indifference. But they all spat out the clogging dust, and cursed the officer who led them.

Farther up the hillside this man ran with the gait of an athlete pushing himself to the limit of endurance. Head down he ran doggedly through the dust and the heat; he ran as though trying to outdistance some merciless pursuer. His eyes were shut tight and he was inhaling from an almost empty reservoir of breath. Captain John Adam was going to run up that mountainside until he could run no more. He was running from last night, and all the nights which still lay ahead. He was running from his own sick self.

Then, almost at the halfway mark, he aimed himself at a patch of bush underneath the cliff and smashed into it headlong. He lay quite still; he had achieved exhaustion: the closest condition to forgetfulness he could ever find.

For Captain John Adam found it unbearable to live with himself and with his future. He had lost his manhood. As an infantry company commander he had drawn daily strength and sustenance from the respect of his fellow fighting men. They knew him as a brave leader, a compassionate man. He had been granted the trust and friendship of men when it is all they have left to give, and this he knew to be the ultimate gift, the highest good. And then, one sun-filled morning, he had forfeited these things for ever. He had cracked wide open; he had cried his fear and panic to the world; he had run screaming from the battle, through the ranks of his white-faced men. He had been sent back here to Volpone in unexpressed disgrace while the authorities decided what to do with him.

Now Captain John Adam rolled over. There was always some supremely unimportant next matter which had to be decided. He lighted a cigarette and gave his whole attention to the small column of climbing smoke. Well, he would sit here until Sergeant Konzuk whipped this miserable, straggling pack up to him, and then he would reveal their next phase of training.

He stood up, a tall young man, looking brisk and competent. His sun-browned face, his blue eyes, the power of his easy movements, even the cigarette dangling negligently from his lips, all seemed to proclaim that here was the ideal young infantry officer.

"Sergeant Konzuk," Captain Adam called now. "Get these

men the hell back to barracks, and leave me alone here!''

The sergeant did not look surprised. He was used to such things by now, and this was no officer to argue with. Sure, he'd take them back to barracks, and let Adam do his own explaining. ''All right, you guys—on your feet!'' said Konzuk. It was no skin to him.

It was late afternoon by the time he had smoked the last of his cigarettes and Adam came down from the mountain. Striding through the camp he frowned with displeasure when he saw the hulking form of Padre Dixon planted squarely in his path. Normally, he knew, he would have liked this big chaplain. There was a sense of inner calm, of repose and reliability about Padre Dixon. Although in his early fifties he had served with devoted competence as chaplain to an infantry battalion. But Adam considered himself to be an outcast, no longer holding any claims upon the men who did the fighting: the men who still owned their self-respect. He made a point of refusing the friendliness which this big man was trying to offer.

''Mind if I walk along with you, son?'' Adam was forced to stop while the Padre knocked his pipe against his boot.

The two men walked on together through the dusk, picking their way between the huts and the barrack blocks. As they neared the officers' mess the Padre stopped and his fingers gripped Adam's arm. He pointed to a small grey hut just within the barbed wire of the camp entrance. ''That's where poor Jones is waiting out his time,'' the Padre said.

''Well?''

The Padre shrugged and seemed busy with his pipe. ''No matter what he's done he's a brave boy, and he's in a dreadful position now.''

''He won't be shot.'' Adam repeated the general feeling of the camp without real interest. ''They'll never confirm the sentence.''

The Padre looked him directly in the face. ''Adam,'' he said. ''It *has* been confirmed. He is going to be executed!''

''No!'' Adam breathed his disbelief aloud. He was truly shocked, and for this instant his own sick plight was forgotten. This other thing seemed so—improper. That a group of Canadians could come together in this alien land for the purpose of destroying one of their own kind...And every day, up at the battle, every effort was being made to *save* life; there were so few of them in Italy, and so pitifully many were being killed every day. This thing was simply—not right.

His eyes sought for the Padre's. "But why?" he asked, with a kind of hurt in his voice. "Tell me—why?"

"The boy's guilty, after all."

"Technically — he was only a witness. And even if he is guilty, do you think this thing is right?"

The Padre could not ignore the urgency in Adam's voice. He spoke at last with unaccustomed sharpness. "No," he said. "It may be something that has to be done—but it will never be right."

The two men looked at one another in the gathering Italian night. For a moment their thoughts seemed to merge and flow together down the same pulsing stream. But then a new idea came to Adam. "Padre," he said. "Why are you telling *me* about this?"

Then they both saw the figure running toward them from the officers' mess. It was Ramsay, the ever-flurried, ever-flustered Camp Adjutant. He panted to a stop in front of them. "Adam," he gasped out. "The Brigadier wants you at once!"

Brigadier Benny Hatfield waited patiently in his office. He liked to feed any new or disturbing thoughts through the mill of his mind until the gloss of familiarity made them less troublesome. Early in his career he had discovered that the calibre of his mind was not sufficiently large for the rank he aspired to, and so deliberately he had cultivated other qualities which would achieve the same end. He emphasized an air of outspoken bluntness, his physical toughness, a presumed knowledge of the way the "troops" thought, and his ability to work like a horse. Indeed the impression he sometimes conveyed was that of a grizzled war horse, fanatic about good soldiering, but with it all intensely loyal, and a very good fellow. His appearance served to support this role:

there was something horselike in the wide grin that lifted his straggling mustache, a grin that proved how affable and immensely approachable he really was.

Now he sat and considered his interview with General Vincent. He understood his superior's unexpressed motives perfectly well: it was a straight question of passing the buck and he intended staying up all night looking after his own interests. This execution was a simple matter of military discipline, after all, and he would ensure that it was carried out in such a way that no possible discredit could reflect on himself. The General, he believed, had made an intelligent choice, and he had an equally good selection of his own in mind. The file of Captain John Adam lay open on his desk.

The Brigadier sat up straight. Ramsay was ushering Captain Adam into his presence.

This was the interview Adam had dreaded since his arrival at the reinforcement base. But he showed no sign now of the sickness and fear that gnawed inside him. He stood at attention while the Brigadier leafed through the file before him.

The Brigadier looked up at last. "Well," he stated. "Captain John Adam." His eyes bored steadily at Adam's face and he waited in silence. He knew that in a moment his unwavering stare would force some betrayal of guilt or inferiority. He waited and at last he was rewarded: the sweat swelled on Adam's forehead, and the man before him felt it essential to break the intolerable silence. "Yes, sir," Adam had to say.

The Brigadier stood up then. "Well," he said again. "It can't be as bad as all that, can it, boy?" His mouth lifted the straggling mustache in a grimace of affability, and despite himself Adam felt a small rush of gratitude.

But then the smile died. "It does not please me," the Brigadier said coldly, "to receive the worst possible reports about you." He consulted the notes on his desk. "You have been AWL twice; there is some question of a jeep you took without permission; and my officers say that you act with no sense of responsibility."

The Brigadier was frowning, his lips pursed. His glance bored steadily at Adam. But then there was a sudden transformation. His smile was reborn in new and fuller glory. "Sit down, boy," he urged. He clapped Adam on the shoulder and guided him into the chair beside his desk.

The Brigadier hitched forward in his seat. Now there was a warmth of friendly concern in his voice. "Adam, boy," he said. "*We* know none of that piddling stuff matters. However —you have read this report from Colonel Dodd?"

It was a needless question. Adam knew the report by memory. It was an "adverse" report: it was the reason why he was back here at Volpone. That piece of paper was his doom. "Not fit to command men in action," it read; "not suitable material for the field". And Colonel Dodd had phrased it as gently as possible; in his own presence he had written it down with pity on his face.

With ungoverned ease his mind slipped back to that sun-filled morning on the Hitler Line. They were walking through a meadow—slowly, for there were Schu mines in the grass—and they moved toward a hidden place of horror: a line of dug-in tank turrets, and mine-strewn belts of wire. And then the earth suddenly erupted with shell and mortar bursts; they floundered in a beaten zone of observed machine-gun fire. A few men got as far as the wire, but none of them lived. There was a regrouping close to the start line, and Adam was ordered to attack again.

The first symptom he noticed was that his body responded to his mind's orders several seconds too late. He became worried at this time lag, the fact that his mind and body seemed about to divide, to assume their own separate identities. Then the air bursts shook the world; no hole in the ground was shelter from the rain of deafening black explosions in the sky above them. Then he remembered the terrible instant that the separation became complete, that he got up and shouted his shame to the world. He got up from his ditch, and he ran blubbering like a baby through his white-faced men. And some of his men followed him, back into the arms of Colonel Dodd.

"Yes," Adam said now, his face white. "I've read the report."

Brigadier Hatfield spoke softly. "If that report goes forward from here you'll be in a bad way — at least returned to Canada for Adjutant General's disposal, some second-rate kind of discharge, the reputation always clinging to you ... " The Brigadier shook his head. "That would be a pity."

If the report goes forward...A pulse of excitement beat in Adam's throat. What did he mean—was there any possibility that the report could be stopped here, that in the eyes of the world he could retain some shreds of self-respect? Adam's breath came faster; he sat up straight.

"Adam!" The Brigadier pounded a fist upon his desk. "*I* have confidence in you. Of all the officers under my command I have selected *you* for a mission of the highest importance."

Adam blinked his disbelief, but the hope swelled strong inside him.

"Yes," the Brigadier said steadily. "*You* are to command the firing squad for the execution of Private Jones!"

Adam blinked again and he turned his head away. For a moment he was weak with nausea the flood of shame was so sour inside him. "No," he heard his voice saying. "I can't do it."

The Brigadier's smile grew broader, and he spoke with soft assurance. "But you can, my boy. But you can." And the Brigadier told him how.

It was all very neatly contrived. Adam had his choice, of course. On the one hand he could choose routine disposal of his case by higher authorities. Colonel Dodd's report, together with Brigadier Hatfield's own statement, would ensure an outcome which, as the Brigadier described it, would cause "deep shame to his family and friends", and Adam was sure of that. On the other hand if he performed this necessary act of duty, this simple military function, then Colonel Dodd's report would be destroyed. He could return to Canada as soon as he desired, bearing Brigadier Hatfield's highest recommendations.

The Brigadier went on to say that the man Jones was a convicted murderer — that Adam should have no scruples on that score; that he relied on his known ability to handle men under difficult circumstances...

Adam listened and each soft word seemed to add to his degradation. This was where the Hitler Line had brought him; this was the inevitable consequence of his lost manhood.

The Brigadier's voice was kindly; his words flowed endlessly like a soft stream of liquid. Then the voice paused. "Of course," the Brigadier said, "it is a task for a determined and courageous man." His glance darted over Adam's bent head and flickered around the room.

Adam broke the silence at last. He spoke without looking up. "All right," he said. "I'll do it."

The Brigadier's response was quick and warm. "Good," he said. "Good *fellow*!" His smile was almost caressing. But to Adam that smile seemed to spread across the horselike face like a stain. The small office and the space between the two men was suddenly close and unbearably warm.

"One more thing, Adam." The Brigadier spoke with soft emphasis. "The members of the firing squad can be detailed later, but your sergeant must be a first-rate man, and — it is most desirable that he be a volunteer. Do you understand?"

Adam forced himself to nod.

The Brigadier stared directly in Adam's face. His voice now rang with the steel of command. "All right," he said. "Bring me the sergeant's name and a draft of your parade orders by 1100 hours tomorrow. Any questions?"

"No, sir." Adam stood up.

"Good boy. Get to it, and remember—I'm relying on you."

"Yes, sir."

The Brigadier leaned back and allowed the smile to possess his face. He had selected exactly the right man for this delicate job: a man of competence who was *bound* to carry the thing through to its final conclusion.

By next morning the news had raced to every Canadian in Italy. At the battle up north men heard about this execution with a dull kind of wonder. Advancing into the attack it was brought to them like bad news in a letter from home; they looked at each other uneasily, or they laughed and turned away. It was not the death of one man back in a place called Volpone that mattered. It was simply that up here they measured and counted their own existence so dear that an unnecessary death, a *planned* death of one of their own fellows seemed somehow shameful. It made them sour and restless as they checked their weapon and ammunition loads.

In the camp at Volpone it was the sole topic of conversation. All officers had been instructed by Brigadier Hatfield to explain to the men that the prisoner, Jones, had been convicted of murder, and therefore had to pay the penalty that the law demanded. But the law was not clear to these men: from their own close knowledge of sudden death they did not understand how a man could commit a murder without lifting a weapon. And those who had seen Private Sydney Jones could not picture that harmless boy as a murderer. Still, the officers went to great pains to explain the legal point involved.

It was soon known that the news had reached the prisoner also, although, to be sure, it did not seem to have changed his routine in the least. All his waking hours were busied with an intense display of military activity. The guard sergeant reported that he made and remade his bed several times a day, working earnestly to achieve the neatest possible tuck of his blanket. The floor was swept five times a day and scrubbed at least once. His battle-dress was ironed to knife-edge exactitude, and his regimental flashes resewn to his tunic as though the smartest possible fit at the shoulder was always just eluding him. At times he would glance at the stack of magazines the Padre brought him, but these were thrown aside as soon as a visitor entered his room. Private Jones would spring to a quiveringly erect position of attention; he would respond to questions with a quick, cheerful smile. He was the embodiment of the keen, alert, and well turned-out private soldier.

The truth was, of course, that Private Jones was a somewhat pliable young man who was desperately anxious to please. He was intent on proving himself such a good soldier that the generals would take note and approve, and never do anything very bad to him. The idea that some of his fellow soldiers might take him out and shoot him was a terrible abstraction, quite beyond his imagination. Consequently Private Jones did not believe in the possibility of his own execution. Even when the Padre came and tried to prepare him Private Jones simply jumped eagerly to attention, polished boots glittering, and rattled off, head high: "Yes, sir. Very good, sir."

A surprising amount of administrative detail is required to arrange an execution. The Brigadier was drawing up an elaborate operation order, with each phase to be checked and double-checked. There were the official witness, the medical officers, the chaplain, the guards, the firing squad, of course; and the conveyance and placing of all these to the proper spot at the right time.

But Captain Adam's first problem was more serious than any of this: his first attempts to recruit the sergeant for his firing squad met with utter failure. After conferring with the Brigadier he decided upon a new approach, and he went in search of Sergeant Konzuk.

The sergeant was lying at ease on his bed reading a magazine. When Adam came in Konzuk scowled. He swung his boots over the side of the bed and he crossed his thick arms over his chest.

Adam wasted no time. "Konzuk," he said. "I want you as sergeant of the firing squad."

The sergeant laughed rudely.

"Never mind that," Adam said. "Wait till you hear about this deal."

"Look," Sergeant Konzuk said. He stood up and his eyes were angry on Adam's face. "I done my share of killing. Those that like it can do this job."

Adam's tone did not change. "You're married, Konzuk. You've a wife and two kids. Well, you can be back in Winnipeg within the month."

Konzuk's mouth opened; his eyes were wide. His face

showed all the wild thoughts thronging through his mind.
The sergeant had left Canada in 1940; his wife wrote him one
laborious letter a month. But his frown returned and his fists
were clenched.

"Look," Konzuk said, fumbling with his words. "This kid's
one of us — see. It ain't right!"

"Winnipeg — within the month."

Konzuk's eyes shifted and at last his glance settled on the
floor. "All right," he said, after a moment. "All right, I'll do
it."

"Good." Adam sought for and held the sergeant's eyes.
"And remember this, Konzuk — that 'kid' is a murderer!"

"Yes, sir."

Then they sat down together. Adam found no satisfaction
in his victory, in the full obedience he now commanded.
Sitting on the iron bed in Konzuk's room they spoke in
lowered voices, and Adam felt as though they were conspir-
ing together to commit some obscene act.

The ten members of the firing squad were detailed the
same day. Adam and Konzuk prepared the list of names and
brought the group to be interviewed by Brigadier Hatfield in
his office. And after that Sergeant Konzuk had a quiet talk
with each man. Adam did not ask what the sergeant said; he
was satisfied that none of the men came to him to protest.

Adam found his time fully occupied. He had installed his
ten men in a separate hut of their own; there were some drill
movements to be practised; and Sergeant Konzuk was drawing new uniforms from the quartermaster's stores. Ten new
rifles had also been issued.

Crossing the parade square that night he encountered
Padre Dixon, and he realized that this man had been avoid-
ing him during the past two days. "Padre," he called out. "I
want to talk to you."

The Padre waited. His big face showed no expression.

"Padre — will you give me your advice?"

The Padre's glance was cold. "Why?" he asked. "It won't
change anything."

And looking into that set face Adam saw that the Padre
was regarding him with a dislike he made no attempt to

conceal. He flushed. He had not expected this. Only days ago this man had been trying to help him.

His anger slipped forward. "What's the matter, Padre — you feeling sorry for the boy-murderer?"

Adam regretted his words at once; indeed he was shocked that he could have said them. The Padre turned his back and started away.

Adam caught at his arm. "Ah, no," he said. "I didn't mean that. Padre — is what I'm doing so awful, after all?"

"You've made your choice. Let it go at that."

"But—my duty..." Adam felt shame as he used the word.

The Padre stood with folded arms. "Listen," he said. "I told you before: no matter how necessary this thing is it will never be right!"

Adam was silent. Then he reached out his hand again. "Padre," he said in a low voice. "Is there no way it can be stopped?"

The Padre sighed. "The train has been set in motion," he said. "Once it could have been stopped — in Ottawa — but now..." He shrugged. He looked at Adam searchingly and he seemed to reflect. "There *might* be one way — ." After a moment he blinked and looked away. "But no — that will never come to pass. I suppose I should wish you good luck," he said. "Good night, Adam."

That meeting made Adam wonder how his fellow officers regarded him. In the officers' mess that night he looked about him and found out. Silence descended when he approached a group and slowly its members would drift away; there was a cleared circle around whichever chair he sat in. Even the barman seemed to avoid his glance.

All right, Adam decided then, and from the bar he looked murderously around the room. All right, *he* would stick by Benny Hatfield — the two of them, at least, knew what duty and soldiering was! Why, what was he doing that was so awful? He was simply commanding a firing squad to execute a soldier who had committed a murder. That's all—he was commanding a firing squad; he was, he was — an executioner!

His glass crashed to the floor. Through all the soft words

exchanged with Brigadier Hatfield, all the concealing eche-
lons of military speech, the pitiless truth now leaped out at
him. He was an executioner. Captain John Adam made a
noise in his throat, and the faces of the other men in the
room went white.

When he left the mess some instinct led him toward the
small grey hut standing at the camp entrance. Through the
board walls of that hut he could see his victim, Jones, living
out his allotted time, while he, Adam the executioner,
walked implacably close by. The new concept of victim and
executioner seized and threatened to suffocate him.

His eyes strained at the Italian stars in their dark-blue
heaven. How had it happened? Only days ago he had regarded the possibility of this execution with horror, as something vile. But now he stood in the front rank of those who
were pushing it forward with all vigor. For an instant his
mind flamed with the thought of asking Brigadier Hatfield to
release him, but at once the fire flickered out, hopelessly.
That night John Adam stayed in his room with the light
burning. He tried to pray.

Brigadier Hatfield had the most brilliant inspiration of his
career: The place of execution would be changed to Rome!
There was ample justification, of course, since the effect on
the troops' morale at Volpone would be bad to say the least.
No one could dispute this, and all the while the Brigadier
relished in imagination the face of General Vincent when he
found the affair brought back to his own doorstep. It only
showed that a regular soldier could still teach these civilian
generals a thing or two!

The Brigadier was in high good humor as he presided at
the conference to discuss this change. All the participants
were present, including one newcomer, an officer from the
Provost Corps, introduced as Colonel McGuire. This colonel
said nothing, but nodded his head in agreement with the
Brigadier's points. His eyes roamed restlessly from face to
face and his cold glance seemed to strip bare the abilities of
every person in the room.

Colonel McGuire, the Brigadier announced, had been in-
strumental in finding the ideal place for the affair. It was a

former Fascist barracks on the outskirts of Rome, and all the —ah, facilities—were readily available. Everyone taking part, and he trusted that each officer was now thoroughly familiar with his duties, would move by convoy to Rome that very afternoon. The execution — here he paused for a solemn moment — the execution would take place at 0800 hours tomorrow morning. Any questions? No? Thank you, gentlemen.

Adam was moving away when the Brigadier stopped him. "John," he called. He had slipped into the habit of using his first name now. "I want you to meet Colonel McGuire."

They shook hands and Adam flushed under the chill exposure of those probing eyes. After a moment the Colonel's glance dropped; he had seen sufficient. As Adam moved off to warn his men for the move he felt those cold eyes following him to the door, and beyond.

Adam kept his eyes closed while Sergeant Konzuk drove. In the back of the jeep Padre Dixon had not spoken since the convoy was marshaled; it was clear that these were not the traveling companions of his choice.

Although Adam would not look all his awareness was centred on a closed three-ton truck which lumbered along in the middle of the convoy. The condemned man and his guards rode inside that vehicle.

The concept of victim and executioner filled Adam's mind to the exclusion of all else. He had tried throwing the blame back to the comfortable politicians sitting at their polished table in Ottawa, but it was no use. He knew that it was *his* voice that would issue the last command. *He* was the executioner...Then another thought came to torment him without mercy: How did his victim, Jones, *feel* now?

They stopped for ten minutes outside a hilltop town, where pink villas glinted among the green of olive trees. Adam followed Padre Dixon to the place where he sat in an orchard. The Padre looked up at him wearily.

"How is he taking it?" Adam demanded at once.

The Padre scrambled to his feet. His eyes flashed with anger. "Who? The boy-murderer?"

"Please, Padre — I've *got* to know!"

The Padre stared at Adam's drawn face. Then he passed a hand across his eyes. "Adam — forgive me. I know it's a terrible thing for you. If it makes it any easier...well, Jones is brave; he's smiling and polite, and that's all. But Adam—the boy still doesn't understand. He doesn't believe that it's really going to happen!" The Padre's voice shook with his agitation.

Adam nodded his head. "That other time, Padre — you said there might be a way of stopping it — ."

"No, forget that — it's too late." The spluttering cough of motorcycles roared between them. "Come. It is time to go." And the Padre laid his hand on Adam's arm.

Adam and Konzuk stood on the hard tarmac and surveyed the site gloomily. The place they had come to inspect was a U-shaped space cut out of the forest. The base of the U was a red-brick wall, and down each side marched a precise green line of cypresses. The wall was bullet-pocked because this place had been used as a firing range, although imagination balked at what some of the targets must have been. On the right wing of the U a small wooden grandstand was set in front of the cypresses. Adam looked around at all this, and then his gaze moved over the trees and up to the pitilessly blue sky above. "All right, Konzuk," he said. "You check things over." And he went away to be alone.

Adam was lying on his bed in the darkness. His eyes were wide open but he made no move when he saw the Padre's big form stumble into his room. Then the Padre stood over his bed, eyes groping for him. He was breathing loudly.

"Adam — he wants to see you!"

"No!"

"You must!"

"I couldn't!" Now Adam sat up in bed. His battle-dress tunic was crumpled. His face was protected by the dark, but his voice was naked.

"No, Padre," he pleaded. "I couldn't."

"Look, son — it's your job. You've no choice. Do you understand?"

There was silence. Adam made a noise in the darkness

which seemed to take all the breath from his body.

"Yes, I understand." He was fumbling for his belt and cap in the dark.

"Padre — what time is it?"

"Twelve o'clock."

"Eight hours."

"Yes."

"Well. Good-by, Padre."

"Good-by, son."

The Provost Sergeant came to attention and saluted. His face was stiff but he could not keep the flicker of curiosity from his eyes. Adam saw that this was a real prison: concrete flooring, steel doors, and iron bars. They stood in what seemed to be a large brightly lit guardroom. A card game had been taking place, and there were coffee mugs, but the guards stood now at respectful attention.

"Where is he?" Adam turned to the Sergeant.

A dark-haired young man stepped from among the group of guards. A smartly dressed soldier, clean and good-looking in his freshly pressed battle-dress. "Here I am, sir," the young man said.

Adam took a step back; he flashed a glance at the door.

The Sergeant spoke then, apologetically. "He wanted company, sir. I thought it would be all right."

"It was good of you to come, sir." This was Private Jones speaking for his attention.

Adam forced himself to return the glance. "Yes," he said. "I mean — it's no trouble. I — I was glad to."

The two men looked one another in the face, perhaps surprised to find how close they were in years. Jones' smile was friendly. He was like a host easing the embarrassment of his guest. "Would you like to sit down, sir?"

"Yes. Oh, yes."

They sat in Jones' cell, on opposite sides of a small table. Because he had to Adam held his eyes on the prisoner's face and now he could see the thin lines of tension spreading from the eyes and at the mouth. It was certain that Jones *now* believed in the truth of his own death, and he carried this fact with quiet dignity. Adam was gripped by a passion of adoration for this boy; he would have done anything for him — he who was his executioner.

"It was good of you to come," Private Jones said again. "I have a request."

Surely, Adam thought, it took more courage to act as Jones did now than to advance through that meadow to the Hitler Line . . .

"Well, sir," Jones went on, his face set. "I'm ready to take — tomorrow morning. But one thing worries me: I don't want you and the other boys to feel bad about this. I thought it might help if I shook hands with all the boys before — before it happens."

Adam looked down at the concrete floor. This was worse than a thousand Hitler Lines; *he knew now he would be able to go back there anytime*. A dim electric-light bulb hung from the ceiling and swayed hypnotically between them. Well, he had to say something. The thing was impossible, of course: he'd never get his men to fire if they shook hands first.

But Jones read the working of his face. "Never mind, sir— maybe you'd just give them that message for me — ."

"I will, Jones. I *will*!"

He stood up; he could not stay here another moment.

Jones said, "Maybe—*you* would shake hands with me?"

Adam stood utterly still. His voice came out as a whisper in that small space. "Jones," he said, "I was going to ask you if I could."

When he came back to the guardroom Adam looked ill. The Provost Sergeant took his arm and walked him back to his quarters.

It was a softly fragrant Italian morning. The dew was still fresh on the grass and a light ground mist rolled away before the heat of the climbing sun. In the forest clearing the neat groups of soldiers looked clean and compact in their khaki battle-dress with the bright regimental flashes gleaming at their shoulders.

The firing squad stood "at ease", but with not the least stir or motion. Sergeant Konzuk was on their right; Captain

Adam stood several paces apart at the left, aligned at right angles to his ten-man rank. The grandstand was filled with a small group of official witnesses. A cordon of military policemen stayed at rigid attention along the top and down each side of the U.

In front of the grandstand stood Brigadier Benny Hatfield, an erect military figure, his stern eye ranging with satisfaction around the precise groupings and arrangements he had ordered. A step behind the Brigadier was Ramsay, his adjutant; then Padre Dixon, and the chief medical officer. The assembly was complete — except for one man.

Somewhere in the background a steel door clanged, a noise which no one affected to hear. Then there came the sound of rapid marching. Three military figures came into view and halted smartly in front of Brigadier Hatfield. Private Jones, hatless, stood in the centre, a provost sergeant on each side. The boy's lips were white, his cheeks lacked color, but he held his head high, his hands were pressed tight against the seams of his battle-dress trousers. It was impossible not to notice the brilliant shine of his polished boots as they glittered in the morning sun.

Brigadier Hatfield took a paper from Ramsay's extended hand. He read some words from it but his voice came as an indistinct mumble in the morning air. The Brigadier was in a hurry. Everyone was in a hurry; every person there suffered an agony of haste. Each body strained and each mind willed: Go! Go! Have this thing over and done with!

The Brigadier handed the paper back to Ramsay with a little gesture of finality. But the three men remained standing in front of him as though locked in their attitudes of attention. Seconds of silence ticked by. The Brigadier's hand sped up to his collar and he cleared his throat with violence. "*Well*, sergeant?" his voice rasped. "Carry on, man!"

"Yessir. Left turn — quick march!"

The three men held the same brisk pace, marching in perfect step. The only sound was the thud of their heavy boots upon the tarmac. They passed the firing squad and halted at the red-brick wall. Then the escorting NCOs seemed to disappear and Private Jones stood alone against his wall. A nervous little smile was fixed at the corners of his mouth.

Again there was silence. Adam had not looked at the marching men, nor did he now look at the wall. Head lowered, he frowned as he seemed to study the alignment of his ten men in a row. More seconds ticked by.

"Captain Adam!"

It was a bellow from Brigadier Hatfield and it brought Adam's head up. Then his lips moved soundlessly, as though rehearsing what he had to say. "Squad," Captain Adam ordered, "Load!" Ten left feet banged forward on the tarmac, ten rifles hit in the left hand, ten bolts smashed open and shut in unison. Ten rounds were positioned in their chambers.

There were just two remaining orders: "Aim!" and "Fire!" and these should be issued immediately, almost as one. But at that moment a late rooster crowed somewhere and the call came clear and sweet through the morning air, full of rich promise for the summer's day which lay ahead.

Adam took his first glance at the condemned man. Jones' mouth still held hard to its smile, but his knees looked loose. His position of attention was faltering.

"Squad!" Adam ordered in a ringing voice, "Unload! Rest!" Ten rifles obeyed in perfect unison.

Adam turned half right so that he faced Brigadier Hatfield. "Sir," he called clearly. "I refuse to carry out this order!"

Every voice in that place joined in the sound which muttered across the tarmac.

The Brigadier's face was deathly white. He peered at Private Jones, still in position against the wall, knees getting looser. He had a split second to carry the thing through. "Colonel McGuire!" he shouted.

"Yes, sir!" McGuire came running toward the firing squad. He knew what had to be done, and quickly. The Brigadier's face had turned purple now; he appeared to be choking with the force of his rage. "Colonel McGuire," he shouted. "Place that officer under close arrest!"

"Sir?" McGuire stopped where he was and his mouth dropped open. Private Jones began to fall slowly against the wall. Then a rifle clattered loudly on the tarmac. Sergeant Konzuk was racing toward the wall and in an instant he had his big arms tight around Jones' body.

"McGuire!" The Brigadier's voice was a hoarse shriek now. "March the prisoner away!"

Padre Dixon stood rooted to the ground. His lips were moving and he stared blindly at Adam's stiffly erect figure. "He found the way!" he cried then in a ringing voice, and he moved about in triumph, although no one paid him attention. At his side Ramsay was spluttering out his own ecstasy of excitement: "Jones will get a reprieve after this! It will have to be referred to London, and then to Ottawa. And they'll never dare to put him through this again — ."

Ramsay looked up as he felt the Padre's fingers bite into his shoulder.

He laughed nervously. "Yes," he chattered on. "Jones may get a reprieve, but Adam's the one for sentencing now." He peered across the tarmac where Adam still stood alone, his face slightly lifted to the warmth of the morning sun. He looked at Adam's lone figure with fear and admiration. "Yes," he said, suddenly sobered. "God help Adam now."

"Don't worry about that, son," said the Padre, starting to stride across the tarmac. "He already has."

Biographical
Notes

Ross, Sinclair

Sinclair Ross, born on a homestead near Prince Albert, Saskatchewan, in 1908, left school after Grade Eleven and began his career working for the Royal Bank of Canada in 1924. Early banking duties took him to different prairie communities and provided background for many of his realistic short stories and novels. An early short story submitted to a British magazine contest won third prize; there were 8000 other entries! His distinguished stories first appeared in *Queen's Quarterly*; later, in 1941, his famous novel of prairie life, *As For Me and My House*, was published. He joined the Royal Canadian Ordnance Corps in the Second World War and saw service overseas. After the war he worked for the bank in Montreal until his retirement in 1968. One of his recent works, *Sawbones Memorial*, was published in 1974. "The Outlaw" is from a collection of early short stories republished in 1968 as *The Lamp at Noon and Other Stories*.

McNamee, James

James McNamee was born in Washington State, but grew up in Victoria, British Columbia. His higher education was terminated early, because, in his words, he "had to withdraw from university to have a series of operations on my head. My friends tell me it was all for nothing." James ranched and farmed in Alberta prior to the Second World War; then he joined the army and was commissioned. After the war he joined the B.C. Forest Service but retired to write short stories and novels. "My Uncle Joe" is the opening section from the novel *Them Damn Canadians Hanged Louis Riel!*, which is likely available in your school library.

Clark, Gregory

Greg Clark, 1892 — 1977, was Canada's best-known storyteller for more than sixty years, during which time he wrote over 4000 daily syndicated newspaper columns and 2000 weekly magazine features. Ernest Hemingway named a son after him; Gordon Sinclair was a *Toronto Star* cub reporter under him. After failing first year at the University of Toronto twice, Greg was invited to leave. He tried to enlist in the First World War, but was rejected because of his height (157 cm) and weight (48 kg in full battle dress). With much perseverance he was enlisted April 1, 1916, as an officer cadet of the 9th Mississauga Horse. His commanding officer offered this explanation for Greg's late arrival in the forces: "It took Greg so long to enlist because he kept getting shoved out of the queue by larger men." Greg entered the action without any formal military experience and learned the art of war in the battlefield. His platoon mates called him "Tom Thumb". At Vimy Ridge he won the Military Cross; the citation read: "He set a fine example of courage and initiative." Greg was one of the last permanent residents of Toronto's King Edward Hotel, where his red vest and tweeds were a familiar sight in the lobby. In 1965 Greg Clark was awarded the Stephen Leacock Medal for Humour for *War Stories*. "The Bully", a true story, is from this collection.

Callaghan, Morley

Morley Callaghan, born in Toronto in 1903, has spent most of his writing life in that city; one notable exception was an eight-month sojourn in Paris, France. While still a student, he held a reporting job for the *Toronto Star* newspaper; Ernest Hemingway, a fellow staff member at that time, encouraged him in his writing. Morley's short stories first appeared in Parisian literary magazines in 1926. The interest of Scott Fitzgerald in Morley's writing resulted in a valuable publishing contact that led to the publication of his first novel, *Strange Fugitive*, in 1928. During this period Morley attended Osgoode Hall law school, and he was called to the bar in 1928. However, he did not practise. The year 1929 saw him in Paris with Hemingway, Fitzgerald, James Joyce, and Gertrude Stein as colleagues. His account of these associations was related in *That Summer in Paris*, published in 1963. He has written many novels, including one you may have read, *Luke Baldwin's Vow*, short stories, and two unpublished plays. A *New York Times* newspaper review once stated, "If there is a better short story writer in the world, we don't know where he is." Callaghan's awards include the Governor General's Award for fiction (1951), the Molson Prize (1969), and the Royal Bank Award for "work that serves humanity". "The Shining Red Apple" is from *Morley Callaghan's Stories*, a retrospective collection published in 1959.

Takashima, Shizuye

Shizuye Takashima, Vancouver-born artist-writer, was fourteen years old in 1942. At war with Japan at that time, Canada invoked the War Measures Act to remove the rights of some 22 000 Japanese-Canadians, the majority of whom were living in British Columbia. Property was seized; brothers were removed to internment camps; fathers were banished to remote camps in the province's interior. Shichan, as she is called by family and friends, graduated from the Ontario College of Art in 1959 and has travelled throughout Europe. Her paintings hang in Canada's museums, and she has had exhibitions in major Canadian galleries. The petite artist turned to writing in 1971; "Exiled" is the opening chapter of her book *A Child in Prison Camp*, describing in words and paintings her wartime experiences, when she, her mother, and her sister were interned in a prison camp. Her story has won a medal from the Association of Children's Librarians, and a Japanese edition has been published. Shichan's philosophy of life is expressed thus: "We're going to the moon. We should be thinking of all that space out there. Once you begin to think of that solar system, you begin to think how ludicrous it is to be fighting here on earth. When are we ever going to learn to live with each other?"

Beresford-Howe, Constance

Constance Beresford-Howe was born in a basement apartment in Montreal in 1922, and, like Eva in the story, lived in the Notre Dame de Grace area. A childhood bout with rheumatic fever required months of bed rest, which "encouraged vices such as music appreciation, reading, writing and introspection". Her first novel, *The Unreasoning Heart*, was published while she was still attending McGill University; the book won the Dodd, Mead Intercollegiate Literary Fellowship. Other novels and short stories followed, along with a teaching career in creative writing. "Running Away from Home" is an excerpt from her best-known work, *The Book of Eve*, published in 1973. Further critical success followed with its 1976 stage adaptation. *The Book of Eve* is itself the first in a series of three linked novels dealing with the stories of three quite different Canadian women. The second novel in this group, *A Population of One*, was published in 1977.

Munro, Alice

Alice Munro was born in Wingham, Ontario, in 1931. Her stories grow from her childhood memories of southern Ontario. She started to write at fourteen, although she was convinced much earlier that she wanted to be a writer: "I never wanted to be anything else since about nine, ever since I stopped wanting to be a movie star." For twenty years she published stories in various literary magazines, but she did not gain wide recognition until 1968 when *Dance of the Happy Shades*, her first published collection of stories, won Canada's highest literary prize, the Governor General's Award. She was the first recipient of the Canadian Booksellers Association—International Book Year Award in 1971—2 for her highly acclaimed novel, *Lives of Girls and Women*. In 1978 she became the first Canadian winner of the Canada —Australia Literary Prize, selected by Australian literary critics. "An Ounce of Cure" is from her 1968 award-winning collection.

Buckler, Ernest

Ernest Buckler was born in 1908 in Dalhousie West, Nova Scotia. He attended Dalhousie University and the University of Toronto. With the exception of five years in Toronto, he has lived and worked all his life on his farm near Annapolis Royal. His literary works include short stories, novels, magazine articles, newspaper columns, radio scripts, and plays. Perhaps his best-known novel is *The Mountain and the Valley*, published in 1952. His awards include the Canada Centennial Medal, 1967, and the Order of Canada, 1974. A modest writer, whose themes are universal, he admits he has "done none of the things which are supposed to constitute an author's apprenticeship. Never hunted walrus in the Arctic, never was a tea taster in Ceylon, never in my life dived for sponges off the coast of Madagascar. About all I'm familiar with is a farm and a pen." "The Wild Goose" originally appeared in 1959 in the *Atlantic Advocate*.

Merril, Judith

Judith Merril, "the first lady of science fiction", was born in New York City in 1923. She began writing science fiction when she was twenty-five, but has held a variety of jobs ranging from busgirl to bookkeeper to ghost writer. The renowned science-fiction writer, anthologist, and critic came to Toronto in 1968, not expecting to stay, "But in the first few weeks, I was utterly astonished — the way people smiled at each other." She did stay and is now a Canadian citizen. Her collection of science-fiction materials began when she was eighteen. In 1970 she donated 5000 items to the Toronto Public Libraries, and these became the base for the Spaced-Out Library, the only known public library in the world exclusively devoted to science fiction. Its growing collection contains novels, short stories, plays, poetry, criticism, periodicals, art, and audio-visual items. Why not plan to visit this unique library at 40 St. George Street when you are in Toronto? The founder, Judith Merril, describes it as "a place for people who are looking for their personal space". The story "Survival Ship" originally appeared in Damon Knight's magazine *Worlds Beyond*.

Laurence, Margaret

Born in Neepawa, Manitoba, in 1926, Margaret Laurence has achieved a respected place in Canadian literature and enjoys a wide audience. Her literary endeavours include novels, essays, short stories, translations, criticism, a children's book, and an autobiographical journal. Two of her novels have won the Governor General's Award for fiction: *A Jest of God* in 1966 and *The Diviners* in 1974. The former became the successful Hollywood film *Rachel, Rachel*. She started writing when she "was about six or seven years old ... small poems, stories and so on. I suppose I would have been about twenty-three when I began to realize that this was really what I wanted to do with my life." Margaret Laurence has been writer-in-residence at the University of Toronto, the University of Western Ontario, and Trent University. "A Queen in Thebes" was published in 1964 in *Tamarack Review*.

Mowat, Farley

Farley Mowat was born in Belleville, Ontario, in 1921, the son of a librarian. He is one of Canada's few professional writers whose livelihood is based upon writing. His university education was interrupted by the Second World War; he spent 1947–8 in the Canadian Arctic prior to finishing his degree in 1949. Mowat began his career in 1952 with *People of the Deer*, a book that established his reputation as an opinionated, crusading writer. His literary output is prolific and varied, encompassing history, ecology, travel, humour, and children's literature. Perhaps you have read *Lost in the Barrens* and *Owls in the Family*; the former won the Governor General's Award for juvenile writing in 1956. He likes writing for younger people; ''Children are simply a better audience. They're open-minded, more receptive than adults.'' The story ''Stranger in Taransay'' appeared in *The Snow Walker* (1975).

Thériault, Yves

Yves Thériault, French Canada's most prolific contemporary author, was born in Quebec City in 1915. He left school at fifteen and held a variety of jobs, including those of truck driver, trapper, and cheese salesman. From 1935 to 1939 he worked as a radio announcer for several Quebec stations, wrote his first radio plays, and published his first short stories. Later jobs were with the National Film Board and Radio–Canada. His literary endeavours also included ''10-cent novels'' written under a pseudonym or anonymously. Since then he has written many novels, short stories, essays, plays, and books for young people in French. Thériault gained international recognition in 1958 for *Agaguk*; this novel won the *Prix de la Province de Québec* and the *Prix France–Canada*. His 1960 novel, *Ashini*, won the Governor General's Award for French fiction and the *Prix France–Canada*; it was translated into English in 1972. ''Akua Nuten'' is from a 1974 collection of Quebec short stories; the translator was Howard Roiter.

Garner, Hugh
Born in 1913, Hugh Garner came to Canada from England with his family when he was six years old, and they settled in the Cabbagetown area of Toronto, then a slum. This became the setting for perhaps his best-known novel, *Cabbagetown*, published in 1950 and revised in 1968. Hugh left school at sixteen to work for the *Toronto Star* newspaper as a copyboy; this marked a lasting association with the world of journalism. During the hungry thirties he rode the rails for some time, finally returning to Toronto. In 1936 he began his formal writing career with the *Canadian Forum*. When the Spanish Civil War broke out in 1936 he volunteered for the Mackenzie–Papineau brigade. During the Second World War he served in both the army and the navy; his naval experiences provided background for his first novel, *Storm Below*, published in 1949. This marked the beginning of a fruitful writing career during which he has produced short stories, essays, and novels. "Red Racer" comes from *Hugh Garner's Best Stories* which won the 1963 Governor General's Award for fiction.

Roberts, Sir Charles G. D.
Sir Charles G. D. Roberts was born in Douglas, near Fredericton, New Brunswick, in 1860, and died in 1943. During his early years he attended university, began to write poetry, was a school headmaster, and taught English, French, and economics at university level. From 1897 to 1907 he lived in New York City with his cousin Bliss Carman. Here he supported himself by writing novels, poetry, and short stories, including his famous collections of animal stories such as *Red Fox*, published in 1905. Later, he moved to England, where, at the outbreak of the First World War, he enlisted in the British Army. In 1916 he transferred to the Canadian Forces Overseas, where he attained the rank of major. After a quarter-century's absence, he returned to Canada and settled in Toronto. In 1926 he became the first recipient of the Lorne Pierce Medal, awarded for distinguished service to

Canadian literature. Roberts was knighted on June 3, 1935. "The Blackwater Pot" was published originally in 1909 in a collection of his stories, *The Backwoodsmen*.

Bird, Will R.

Will Bird was born in East Mapleton, Nova Scotia, in 1891, "when Queen Victoria still had ten years left to reign". For distinguished service in the First World War, he was awarded the Military Medal. Indirectly, the war led to his prolific writing career. He had been gassed at Mons and was convalescing in a Halifax hospital when he read of a newspaper contest offering $25 for the best fish story. He dictated the story to his wife, submitted it, and won. The editor offered Will a job as a roving reporter visiting parts of the province and writing articles about local people and events. His writing, although part-time, was prolific (he was employed by the Nova Scotia Bureau of Information). He has published over twenty-five books, which include many historical romances and over five hundred short stories. His best-known collection was published in 1946 as *Sunrise for Peter*. "The Weasel Skin" is from a later collection of his short stories entitled *Angel Cove* (1972).

Raddall, Thomas

Thomas Raddall, born in Hythe, England, came to Halifax, Nova Scotia, when he was ten years old. He left school at fifteen, after his father was killed in action at Amiens in the First World War, and enlisted as a wireless operator. After four years' service on ships and coastguard stations in Nova Scotia, he turned to bookkeeping and accountancy for his livelihood. It was during this period that he began to write short stories for publication in American and British magazines. In 1938, Raddall became a full-time professional writer, supporting himself solely by his literary output — a great achievement in Canada at that time. The following year his first collection of short stories was published. Raddall has since attained international recognition as a skilled writer of stories, novels, and histories; several of his works have been translated into French. He has won three Governor General's Awards (1943, 1948, 1957), the Lorne Pierce Medal (1956), and the Order of Canada Medal of Service, and was elected to the Royal Society of Canada. "Triangle in Steel" first appeared in *Maclean's* magazine and was later reprinted in a 1945 collection, *Tambour and Other Stories*. A true artist, Raddall would not compromise his craft for success as a popular writer. Dissatisfied with the conclusion of his first draft of "Triangle in Steel", he left the story for several years until "I sat down one evening, looking over my old notes, and the whole thing came to me."

Wilson, Ethel
Ethel Wilson was born in Port Elizabeth, South Africa, in 1890, and was raised in England. When she was eight years old, after her parents' death, she emigrated to Vancouver to live with her mother's family. She taught school in Vancouver until her marriage in 1920. In 1937, magazines began to publish her short stories; these were later reprinted in *Mrs. Golightly and Other Stories* (1961), from which "Hurry, Hurry" is taken. Her first novel, *Hetty Dorval*, was not published until she was fifty-seven years of age; its success was followed by that of others, including *Swamp Angel* (1954). Ethel Wilson was awarded the Lorne Pierce Medal in 1964 and the Order of Canada Medal of Service in 1970.

McDougall, Colin
Colin McDougall, born in Montreal in 1917, graduated from McGill University in 1940 and then joined the army, where he achieved distinction. Awarded the Distinguished Service Order, he attained the rank of major. Since that time he has held various administrative positions at McGill University. His short stories were published in several magazines. In 1953 "The Firing Squad" won first prize in a fiction contest

sponsored by *Maclean's* magazine, and also the University of Western Ontario President's Medal for the year's best short story by a Canadian. This story later evolved into his novel, *Execution*, which itself won the Governor General's Award for fiction in 1958.

97 08 18 28 38 48 58 68 BP 9 8 7 6 5 4 3